Canine Form Follows Function
Separating Fact from Fiction

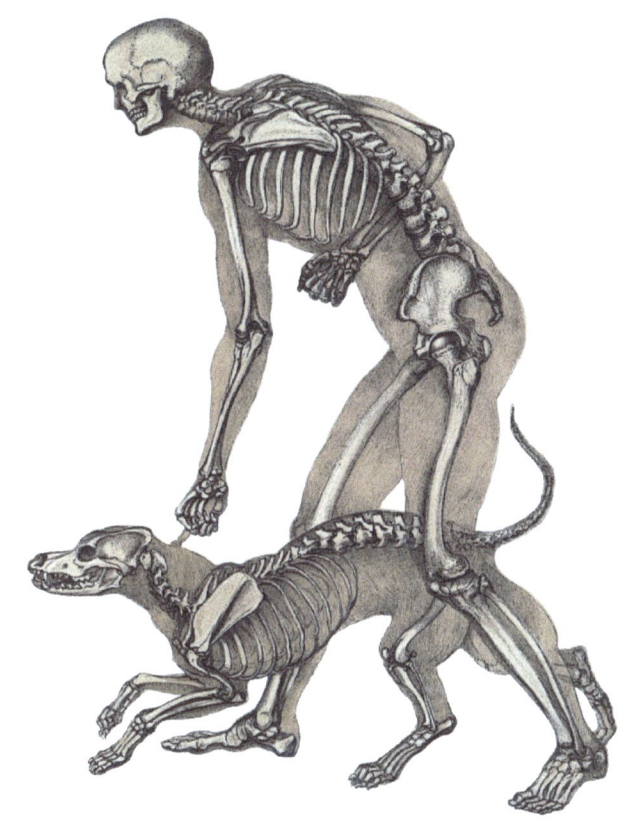

by Jeanne Joy Hartnagle-Taylor
Edited by Tracy Libby

Copyright © 2021 Jeanne Joy Hartnagle-Taylor

All rights reserved. No part of this book may be used or reproduced in any manner whatsoever, including electronic media, Internet, or newsletters, without written permission from the publisher.

ISBN – 978-1-7336742-3-2
BISAC: PET004010 Pets / Dogs / Breeds
Printed in the United States

Dedication

This book is dedicated to my circle of friends and acquaintances
who have kindly supported my work through the years;
to the memory of my brother Joe who taught me how to use a computer,
and
Dr. R. Harrison Smythe, a brilliant veterinary surgeon.

Table of Contents

1	Relating Form to Function	Page 01
2	The Blueprint	Page 05
3	Dog Architecture	Page 15
4	Neck, Topline and the Body	Page 33
5	The Forequarters	Page 47
6	The Hindquarters	Page 67
7	The Gait	Page 83
8	The Head	Page 99
9	Longevity	Page 111

Foreword

I can't remember a time when dogs were not a part of my life. With the exception of a purebred Bichon Frise, which my parents traded a set of encyclopedias for when I was five years old, most of my dogs were mixed breeds. Adorable mutts. In 1985, I acquired my first purebred Australian Shepherds — a black tri bitch (Art Blackford, Winchester Kennels) and a blue merle dog (Becky deLeon, Somercrest Australian Shepherds). I was hooked!

In 1989, when Jeanne Joy Hartnagle-Taylor's book *All About Aussies: The Complete Handbook of Australian Shepherd Dogs* was published, it became my bible, my go-to book for everything Aussie—along with the 1996 follow-up *All About Aussies: The Australian Shepherd from A to Z*.

I first met Jeanne Joy in the early 1990s when I showed my blue merle bitch under her in the BBX class. She gave us Reserve Winners Bitch, and after the show we chatted briefly. Through the years, I had the opportunity to show under her several times, and we have since become friends—chatting for hours, at every opportunity, about canine structure, movement, genetics, breeding, and pretty much everything dog related.

I am honored to write the foreword for her newest book, *Canine Form Follows Function: Separating Fact from Fiction*, her 10th book in an impressive collection of topnotch publications. Jeanne Joy has not only written this book, she has lived it.

She has spent a lifetime working, training, and handling farm and ranch dogs. As the third generation of Hartnagles to train and work stockdogs in the demanding and often dangerous environment on farms and ranches, she is uniquely qualified to discuss functional anatomy. Her profound experience and expertise come from actual first-hand experience.

Many of you know Jeanne Joy's parents, Elaine and Ernest Hartnagle, who founded Las Rocosa Australian Shepherds in 1955, which went on to become the #1 Hall of Fame Kennel, and the #1 Hall of Fame Excellent Kennel. For more than 60 years they developed a distinct bloodline and were a major force in the breed. They had a sound knowledge of dogs (and horses) under working conditions. Sadly, something many dog owners today have not experienced. Jeanne Joy continues her parents' legacy by continually sharing her knowledge of canine structure, movement, and functionality.

This book, as are her others, is a testament to a canine-savvy person who is eager to share her knowledge in order to help others excel by better understanding functional anatomy for performance and working dogs.

Jeanne Joy does not delve into the finer points of breed judging. There are plenty of books that tackle that topic. She does, however, focus on the structure, functional anatomy, and physiology that enable working and performance dogs to excel, be it in obedience, herding, tracking, retrieving, or agility. And, yes, even in the breed ring.

Not only is this book wonderfully written, complete with umpteen illustrations, anatomical drawings, and photographs, it provides an in-depth analysis and breakdown of canine structure and debunks countless myths that have long been accepted as truth. The big one being that all dogs, regardless of their breed, size, or the purpose for which they were originally bred, will move in the same manner. What is the old adage that if you repeat something enough times it becomes truth?

Dogs were originally bred for a specific purpose and function—hunting, guarding, swimming, going to ground, retrieving, etc., —and they varied in their ability to sprint, trot, turn, stop, and accelerate based upon the proportions and structure that best allowed them to perform their job. Jeanne Joy shows us how and why structure improves or, in many cases, impedes movement and function.

Indeed, the world of canine structure is often subjective — when it should not be. The tried and true axiom, "movement tells all" is as significant today as it was 100 years ago.

For anyone who works, trains, or has an interest in dogs, I hope you will follow Jeanne Joy on this continuous journey as she shares her insight into functional anatomy, structure, and movement.

~ Tracy Libby
Award-winning freelance writer and photographer; recipient of the Alliance of Purebred Dog Writers Arthur F. Jones Award of Excellence; recipient of numerous Dog Writers' Association of America Maxwell Awards; author of 14 books on canine history and training; Owner/handler, trainer of Australian Shepherds for 36 years, exhibiting in agility, conformation and obedience.

Introduction

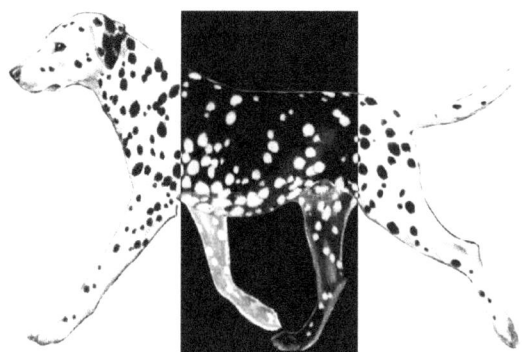

The greater majority of the books about structure and gait are from a conformation, show-ring perspective with a lot of discussion about reach and drive. It reminds me what Louis L'Amour once said about historians, "Historians follow the main line. One historian follows another one, adding maybe a detail here and there or questioning something the other fella has said. They don't go off to the right and left and they don't go out there in the boondocks to see what was happening." I didn't want to do that.

This book wasn't written to address the fine points of breed judging nor is it an exhaustive study of structure and movement. My focus is on functional anatomy for working and performance dogs. The type of physiology that enables difficult turns with sudden stops and starts for dogs at work and play. I am hoping *Canine Form Follows Function* will allow readers to see their dog in a slightly different light.

One of the topics I hope you'll find of interest is my discussion on the pacing gait. Is there a genetic basis for some dogs to pace and not others? Is pacing the result of fatigue or a physical weakness? Or is pacing determined by motor neurons in the spinal cord that control flexor and extensor muscles?

I think you'll enjoy and learn from the comments from my guest contributors including Carol Ann Hartnagle, Michael J. Ryan, Steve Shope and Tanya Wheeler. I want to give a special thank you to Tracy Libby for her impeccable work, encouragement and lovely photographs.

Many of the pictures I've chosen to illustrate this book are moderate examples of different breeds from earlier decades. In addition, there are a number of Australian Shepherds pictured throughout the book. It's a breed I've known and studied since childhood. You may see some pictures you've seen before. They just happen to be a good example of the point I'm trying to explain. I am so pleased to include Herrmann Dittrich's gorgeous anatomical illustrations. They are not only a work of art in themselves, they provide external and beneath-the-skin drawings of skeletal structure and musculature.

Please note: The beautiful drawings of the Beauceron used throughout the book by Hermann Dittrich (who was a German medical illustrator) were done in a time before ear cropping and tail docking were banned in Europe. Likewise, the dog is uniquely posed in a natural stance rather than a traditional show pose.

Author's note: Agility unless specifically referenced as a performance sport refers to the dog's nimbleness.

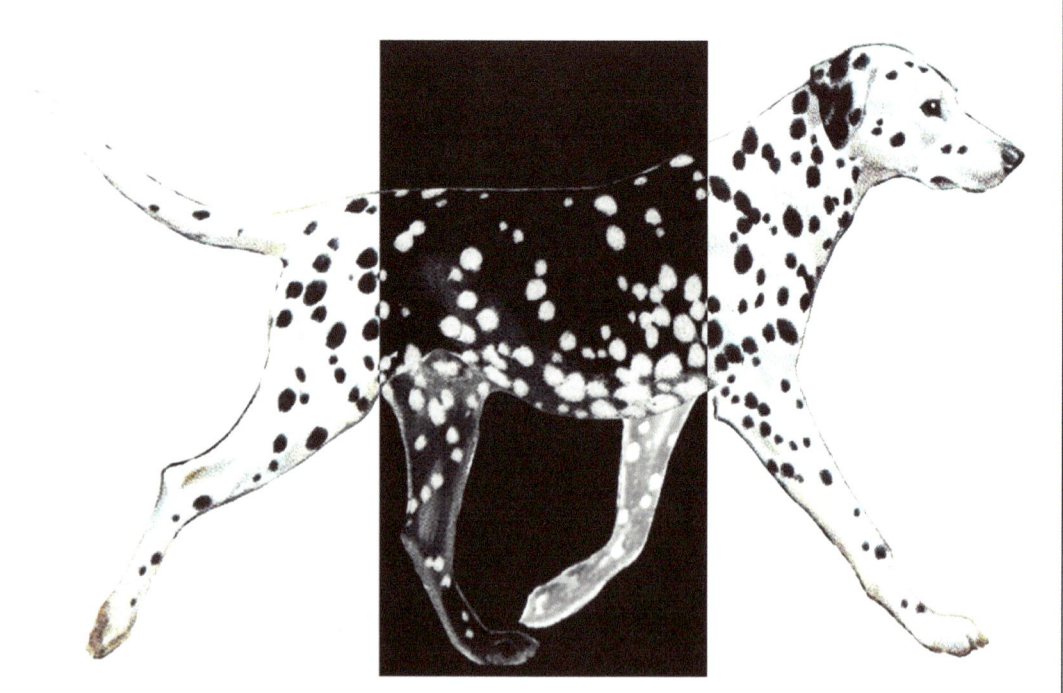

1 Relating Form to Function

As breeds evolve, one of the first things to change is the head.

An attractive, moderate Bull Terrier (above) that was typical of the 1930s.

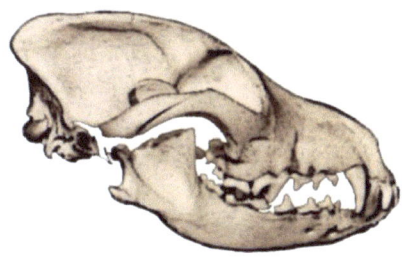

Compare the head and skull of the 1930s era Bull Terrier to the one below from only two decades later.

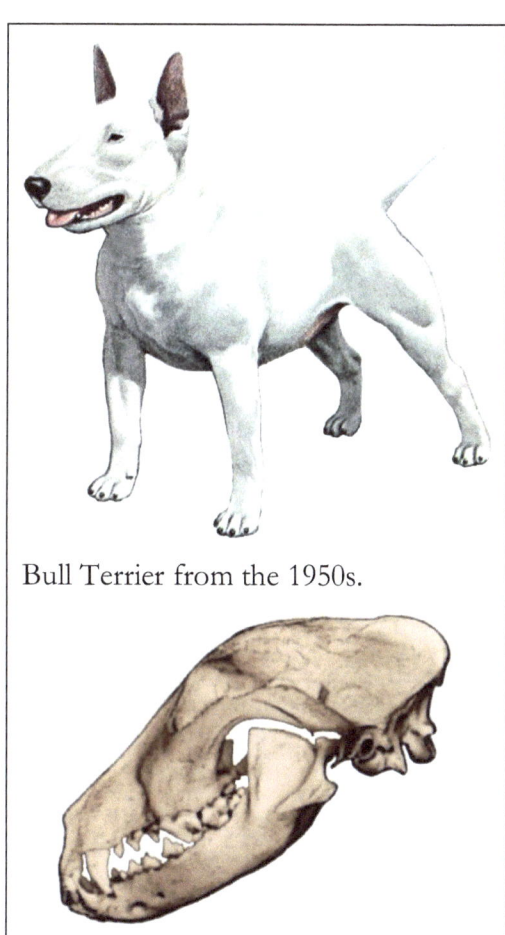

Bull Terrier from the 1950s.

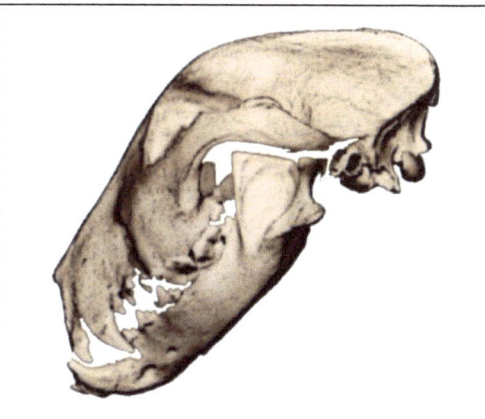

A Bull Terrier skull typical of the 1970s illustrating the dorsoventral nose bend.

The saying "form follows function" is an adaptation of "form ever follows function" as it appeared in the article, *The Tall Office Building Artistically Considered* and is credited to Louis Sullivan, an American architect who coined the phrase. He believed the shape of a building or object should primarily relate to its intended function or purpose. He implied that the function should be the primary concern of anyone designing objects.

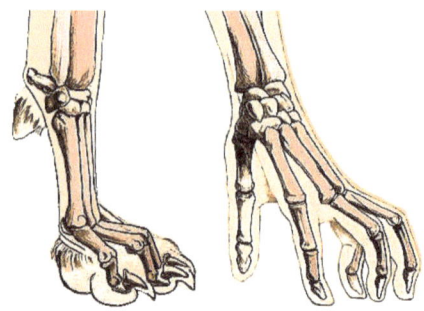

In biology, form follows function means that the form and shape of a body structure goes hand in hand to the purpose or function of that structure. Namely, the function of a body part dictates the shape of that body part. For example, compare your wrist and hand to the dog's "wrist and hand." While the bones of the two are homologous, the parts serve different functions and their forms have adapted to follow that function.

As expected, the hindlimb muscles of the hare are functionally similar to those observed in other quadrupeds including dogs and horses. Nonetheless, the muscle-tendon architecture varies noticeably between species and breeds that are adapted for different locomotor functions. The practical specialization of the muscle-tendon architecture within the pelvic limbs is seen in the hare, as in other species that require fast running, accelerating quickly with lightning-fast changes in direction.

The principle of form follows function as it relates to dog breeds is thought to be the result of its heritage. Compare the fleet-footed Greyhound to the American Staffordshire Terrier, which at the opposite end of the spectrum is built for strength. The Greyhound's long, thin legs are adapted for high speed running. They have aerobic stamina at the sprint. Whereas the American Staffordshire Terrier's proportionately shorter, thicker bones are designed to accommodate a larger body mass.

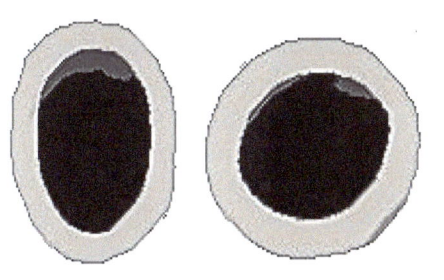

The cross section of the humerus from a Greyhound (left) and a cross section from an American Staffordshire Terrier (right).

What genetic research has proven is that certain traits are coupled or linked together with one or more traits and cannot be passed on in isolation. For example, the width of the leg bone and the length of the skull are controlled by the same group of genes. If one trait is changed, the coupled trait changes too. An example is the anatomical changes that took place in silver foxes as they were selected for sociability, carried out at the Russian Academy of Sciences in Novosibirsk.

Foxes selected for tameness frequently exhibited a loss of pigmentation (variation in skin and coat color), juvenilized facial and body features, floppy ears, curly tails, shorter limbs, and malocclusion of the lower jaw, as well as a decrease in cranial height and width. They had shorter and wider muzzles than their wild counterparts, akin to the differences between the skulls of dogs and wolves.

The dog's skull, pelvis shape, and ribcage, and the position of their limbs indicate whether a dog is built for speed or strength. A cross section of the long bones - humerus and the femur - reveal the shape (either oval or round) and thickness of the shaft. For example, a cross-section of the middle of the upper arm shaft in the Greyhound is elliptical and in the American Staffordshire Terrier it's round with a thicker shaft. Interestingly though, the upper arm is approximately the same proportional length in all dogs.

In their research article for the Journal of Experimental Biology, *Functional trade-offs in the limb bones of dogs selected for running versus fighting,* T. J. Kemp, K. N. Bachus, J. A. Narin, D. R. Carrier, concluded there can be a real conflict between the two functions of the Greyhound (running) and the pit bull (fighting). "Both locomotion and fighting are critical to survival and reproductive fitness in many species, but traits that make an individual good at fighting may, in many cases, limit locomotor performance and vice versa. Generally, this type of trade-off can be expected because rapid and economical terrestrial locomotion is dependent on long, gracile limbs and muscles that are specialized for the storage and recovery of elastic strain energy (Hildebrand and Goslow, 2001; Taylor, 1994), whereas specialization for fighting appears to be associated with short, stout limbs and muscles specialized for high force production."

The study concerning trade-offs in limb bones goes on to state, "In a study, comparing the architecture of limb muscles of a breed of domestic dog specialized for running with that of a breed specialized for fighting, we found that running breeds had relatively less muscle mass distally in their limbs, weaker muscles in their forelimbs, but stronger muscles in their hindlimbs, and a greater capacity for elastic storage in their muscle-tendon systems."

Huskies, but they are airborne about 75 percent of the time using a double suspension gallop. Being inflight while trying to pull a sled wouldn't work out well because the sled would pull them back every time they were midair.

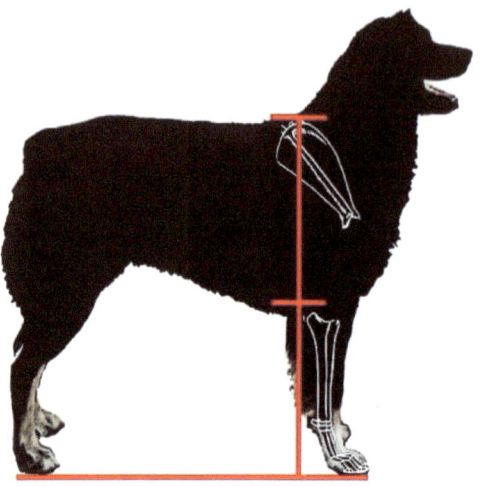

Compare the way an Alaskan Husky needs to sprint when pulling a sled to the way a Greyhound sprints. Huskies are built for speed and strength. They use a single suspension gallop in order to pull the sled while running. Greyhounds are far faster than

"The legginess ratio is very useful in the study of speed, endurance or agility," in *Dog Locomotion and Gait Analysis*, Curtis Brown defined the ratio of trunk height to free leg length below the trunk.

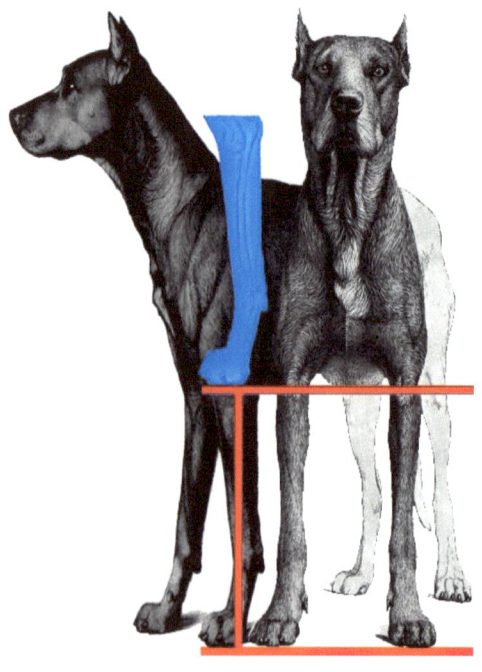

2 The Blueprint

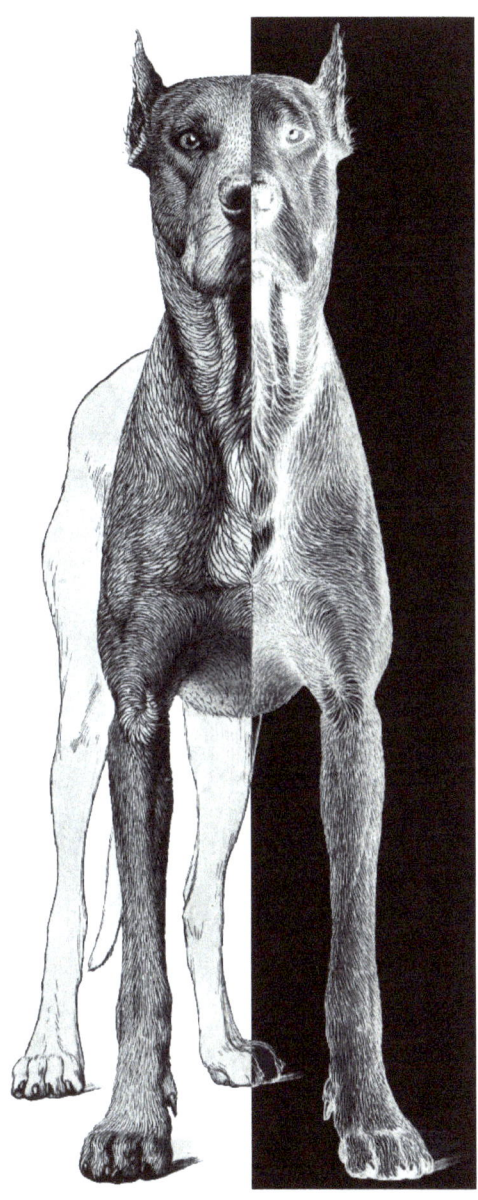

A breed standard is the blueprint, a written description for breeders and judges to evaluate against. Is the dog fit for the function?

In the beginning, the authors of breed standards tried to describe the type of dog ideally suited for the job description as it then existed. At the same time understanding the only real method of testing the form is the function which further reveals the character and determination needed for the work.

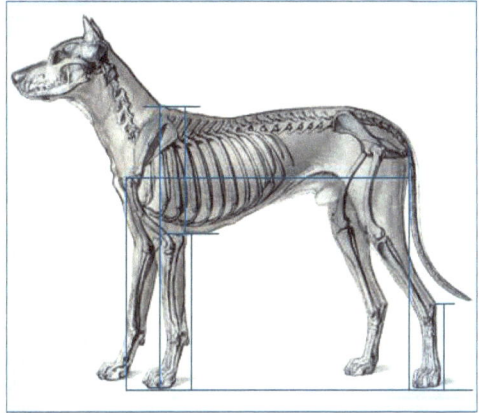

A breed's foundation—its original purpose—is thought to be the baseline for their structure and temperament. For example, the original purpose of a racing greyhound or working stockdog is reflected in its overall type.

Upland game hunters like the English Springer Spaniel (above) require stamina, speed and the skill to crash through deep and punishing cover like these tangled briers.

The Chesapeake Bay Retriever and Labrador Retriever were bred for hunting, a task that required them to run out to retrieve waterfowl and return nonstop to the hunter, regardless of the landscape.

Even though the Dalmatian is meant to keep up with a carriage, it was not developed to move with the kind of agility that stockdogs need.

Cattle can be dangerous to work. Cowdogs like the Australian Shepherd take a lot of hard knocks. They are managing animals that weigh ten times what they do.

Stockdogs require quick bursts of speed to sprint ahead, stop abruptly, with a simultaneous rollback to turn back escaping livestock, and then drop down low enough to avoid being kicked.

Australian Cattle Dogs were bred to gather and herd cattle sometimes scattered over hundreds of acres, requiring them to be extremely agile, fleet of foot to keep the animals together regardless of the erratic behavior of the cows or changes in terrain of the land.

The Kelpie, a superior sheep dog developed in the outback of Australia, must be fleet footed to nimbly sprint over the backs of sheep, as pictured below.

By comparison, a brawny Alaskan Malamute's feet must have longer contact—power originates when the foot is in contact with the ground—to pull the weight for heavy freighting across the brutal landscape of the Arctic.

The lighter Alaskan and Siberian Huskies are the swiftest and able to carry lighter loads for long distances in the frozen tundra of the far North country.

A Border Collie using athleticism and the power of its keen eye to stop wild and difficult Australian Merino sheep in their tracks.

Separating Fact from Fiction

Certain breed standards and books theorize that herding and droving dogs are long distance trotters that need to be able to cover as much ground as possible with as few strides as necessary. Therefore, they require a sustained trotting assembly.

In the days before motorized transport and railways, herding dogs were essential to move any number of cattle, sheep, goats, pigs, and even geese for great distances over untamed land and sometimes water. Droving required stamina and force with the temperament to move stubborn or anxious animals along the wild countryside and through crowded towns. The work required flexibility. The dog had to be able to work any position relative to the stock—pushing from the rear, going to the head to turn the group, and thwarting breakaway attempts from any point in the herd or flock.

The job description required a dog to use many gaits from a walk to a sprint. They may trot for certain distances as well as make instantaneous gait changes, quick and sudden turns, and abrupt stops over varied terrain.

Not only do ranch dogs use varied gaits, they also have to be proficient swimmers.

It has long been known that a good dog can accomplish more than four or five of the best cowhands when it comes to handling cattle in difficult situations in big rough country. Terry Sanders, a Cattleman ranching along the Trinity River in Texas described, "One spring, a flash flood caught a sizeable bunch of cattle in the river bottom. Instead of heading for the hills, the cattle climbed up on the first knoll they came to, and stood there bawling while the water got deeper and deeper." Sanders said, "Little Bruce [uncle] hauled a row boat to the edge of the water in a wagon. He put three English Shepherds in it and rowed into the water and started for shore. The dogs swam from cow to cow, nipping at tails, hips and backs, anything they could get hold of. One old cow started after the boat, and soon the whole bunch was swimming for safety. The dogs stayed behind them until every [cow] was ashore."

In a similar situation on the Casa de Carrillo ranch that was located on very rough coastal terrain of Marin County in northern California, an Australian Shepherd named Cookie, owned by our dear friends the Carrillos, saved seventeen heifers out of the flooded Laguna de Santa Rosa river, the largest tributary of the Russian River, by swimming them to high ground during a winter flood. She swam through the raging water to save the group of yearlings that had gotten stranded on a small island.

In order for herding dogs to perform this type of work, dogs must be built to sprint suddenly. In other words, they must be able to transition from a trot to a sprint automatically.

Separating Fact from Fiction

So, from where did the idea that today's herding dogs are supposed to be sustained trotters come? More than likely it came from tending, a common practice throughout Europe. It's a supervised type of grazing in unfenced, dynamic areas where the dogs act as living fences. The shepherd or herder keeps their animals safely contained within an established perimeter and while moving their livestock from one place to another with the help of their dog(s).

In Germany and other parts of central Europe, stock is grazed in fallow areas among fields of crops. Sheep are allowed to forage strips of grass between crops. Active boundary work is required when a large flock is grazed in more cultivated areas, at the edge of an unfenced field and when grazing the narrow area along a roadside.

A painting of a true working German Shepherd Dog (GSD) from proven herding bloodlines that is moderate and balanced.

In the tending style of managing livestock, the shepherd and his dogs are required to keep the stock out of cultivated areas or straying into adjoining fields. The dog's job is to patrol the perimeter and push back or *ward off* any animal that tries to cross it. Once the shepherd indicates the boundary, the sheep may come up to the edge, but the dog will not let them go beyond it.

Margelen's Chieftain UDT, better known as Topper, 1953's National Obedience Champion. Topper was a beautiful example of a moderate, athletic German Shepherd loping across a field.

Trotting up and down the edge of a meadow to keep the sheep in their designated grazing area comes naturally to German Shepherd Dogs. Other breeds, such as the Briard and Bouvier des Flandres with good territorial instincts are also used for tending, but they are generally more relaxed in their approach. Rather than continually moving along the boundary, they keep a watchful eye on the flock grazing. They move only as necessary to keep the livestock in the perimeter.

The Changing Structure of Breeds

Abnormalities sneak in and are then unintentionally perpetuated, such as in the beloved Bulldog. Just as genetic traits are linked together, so too are mutations. A mutation in one of the master genes usually has drastic consequences because it affects not just one gene, but a whole gene cascade. It was believed, and often cited, a Bulldog's pushed-in face with the upturned nose and undershot jaw allowed them to breathe better while hanging onto a bull. Instead, they suffer from brachycephalic airway obstructive syndrome, which can lead to severe respiratory distress.

We have only to look at the German Shepherd Dog to see the genetic manipulation by humans. Breeders have so changed the look of this amazing breed it's difficult to imagine them capable of performing their original function. We see dogs with excessive angulation, trotting with their rear pasterns almost flat on the ground, which would render them unfit for herding sheep especially in the high mountain country. "No counterpart of this gait is seen in the wild; it is a man-created trot essentially performed as part of an exaggerated flying trot," wrote Curtis Brown.

When I was in Germany in the early 1990s, I had the opportunity to see actual working German Shepherd Dogs and Old German Herding Dogs, the Altdeutsche Hütehunde, in the fields performing their inherited function as they have for centuries.

When we stop looking at the dogs through the lens of its original purpose, be it herding, hunting, retrieving, etc., we will have created in time a distinctly different breed. We can see this happening to a number of breeds, such as Australian Shepherds, Border Collies, and Golden Retrievers, which is why performance dogs look different than their conformation cousins that are no longer able to perform their historical function (instinct aside).

False Supposition

Dr. Reginald Harrison Smythe, who was an examiner in surgery to the Royal College of Veterinary Surgeons from 1937 to 1959 stated, "The racing Greyhound is, as compared with the exhibition type, almost straight in hock and stifle and covers far less ground. When raced, the one against the other, the little straight-legged dog can run away from the over-angulated show dog owing to the fact that it is less wasteful to employ a shorter, straighter hind limb and a greater number of shorter strides than to employ a smaller number of longer strides.

He said, "Angulation was introduced on a false supposition but once it had become established it was retained because it gave a more pleasing appearance to the dog's outline."

Dr. Smythe pointed out, "When the tibia becomes longer, with the hind feet well behind the body, the muscle mass covering the pelvis becomes less, since the muscles are not exercised as formerly as they were, and the muscles now mainly employed are the gastrocnemius behind the limb, and the rectus femoris and vasti in front of it. These give rise to increased joint movement between the head of the femur and the cup of the acetabulum, but the muscle mass overlying the joint, and keeping its parts in apposition, is less in the over-angulated dog than in the normal limb."

Separating Fact from Fiction

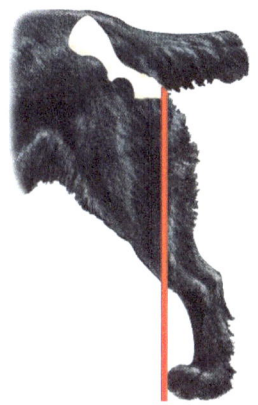

To check the balance of the rear assembly, drop a plumb line from the caudal or rearmost point of the dog's buttocks (ischial tuberosity) to the ground. The misconception is the line will drop in front of the toes of a well-structured dog. In the breed ring, many breeders and judges mistakenly believe this is the balance point required for proper movement. Furthermore, they believe when the plumb line drops through the vertical line of support behind the toes to the metatarsal pad, the dog lacks angulation and will have restricted movement.

The reality is, "Excessive pelvic limb angulation requires tremendous muscular strength and coordination to stabilize the rear end - more strength and coordination is needed to effectively use the hind limbs for locomotion," Amy Watson MA VetMB MRCVS CCRT CVA (IVAS) wrote in her blog post, *Crufts Conundrum*, "This has the effect of making these dogs less accurate with placing their hind feet and they struggle with making sharp turns. Whilst they seem to get less injuries due to torque, they are more prone to injuries due to hyperextension."

When more muscle strength is required because of increased angulation it builds up heat and accelerates fatigue.

The Beloved St. Bernard

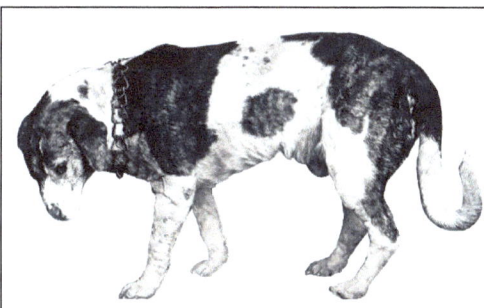

Barry dr Menschenretter, also known as Barry (1800 - 1814), the original St. Bernard, as he appeared on display at the Natural History Museum of Bern.

Believe it or not, the St. Bernard was developed from cow herding dogs known as Alpine Mastiffs. The most famous, of course, is Barry. He is credited for saving 40 exhausted travelers during his lifetime in the treacherous St. Bernard Pass on the Swiss-Italian border.

After losing many of their valuable breeding dogs in avalanches while they were performing mountain rescues during the severe winters from 1816 to 1818 - the monks of the St. Bernard hospice crossed the moderate Barry-type dogs with the Newfoundland.

What resulted were dogs with thick coats inclined to gather snow clumps that weighed them down and significantly reduced their stamina.

In 1923, Barry's body and skull were modified by a taxidermist to match the Saint Bernard of that era. Although brandy kegs were never actually carried in rescue work, Barry is displayed with a keg for the benefit of visitors.

The Australian Shepherd

The Australian Shepherd is a good example of changing structure. In 1977, the Australian Shepherd Club of America (ASCA) adopted a breed standard that was in use for more than 40 years. In that period of time, a distinct kind of Australian Shepherd emerged from the early foundation ranch dogs with their original sprinting structure. The standard aided by the show program saw the development of Aussies with trotting drive trains.

What did that mean for the breed? Not all Australian Shepherds are created equal. The dog's ability to transition from a trot to a sprint is genetic and linked to certain body types, which is not surprising since genetic research has already proven that traits are coupled.

Although most Aussies have the same basic appearance that sets them apart from other breeds, there is a distinct difference between the basic structure and trotting style of the working bloodlines and those bred for the conformation ring. A similar comparison can be drawn between the differences of the quick turning Quarter Horse and the Standardbred able to trot or pace at a high speed without breaking gait.

My father, Ernie Hartnagle, the legendary Australian Shepherd breeder who played an outsized role in the breed's development and growth, said, "The formation of the trotting Aussie produced a dog that could move effortlessly for long distances. The trade-off for this development was paid for with the sacrifice of supreme agility necessary to outrun and turn sheep and cattle. The longer extension of gait naturally produces a slower reaction time to negotiate changes of direction." A dog with the trotting drive train requires an extra stride to alter gaits or change direction.

Sorting, penning, and turning back livestock often require rapid accelerations, sharp turns, and abrupt stops at full speed. Also required are roll backs and simultaneous lead changes. After which the dog must return to a "flat out" run again in two strides in a different direction. All the while, dodging flying hooves and lethal horns.

This primary work cannot be accomplished with the sustained trotting style that is enhanced through show ring pageantry, but must be accomplished at different gaits from a walk or trot to a sprint.

Trotters and Sprinters

That is to say, the greater angulation of the drivetrain built for sustained trotting produces fewer strides per 100 feet than the sprinting drivetrain does at the same gait. Simply put, while the trotter is in the process of completing the first stride, the sprinter is in its second stride. The trotting dog spends more time in the air due to the longer stride, which produces a slower reaction time. The sprinter, however, with his shorter stride is more agile and can make abrupt changes in direction much quicker.

Canine athletes also depend on the sprinting drivetrain for maximum efficiency to function as a herder or hunter. The trot to sprint transition is significant in a dog's ability to function as a hunter or herder and excel in performance events, such as Agility, Flyball or Frisbee that require quickness, good jumping ability, and turn around efficiency. (See page 95 for more discussion on the trot to sprint transition.)

A foundation Aussie and a natural born sprinter, works sheep along a ridge. The zoomed in picture above perfectly captures the transition from a ***trot to a sprint.***

Trotting Drivetrain	Sprinting Drivetrain
More shoulder layback.	Moderate shoulder. A little less slope to front pasterns.
The hock and plantar pads are out behind ischium.	The hock and plantar pads are under the ischium.
Flatter croup	**Steeper croup**
Shorter hocks (Metatarsi).	**Longer hocks** (Metatarsi).
Longer strides at the trot.	Shorter, quicker strides at the trot.
Dogs with the **trotting** drivetrain are able to take longer strides with their legs covering more ground but are slower making gait changes.	Dogs with the **sprinting** drivetrain are more exact when placing their feet and are able to turn more sharply than dogs with the trotting drivetrain.
Up and down, rocking horse running style, bouncy.	**Forward, ground covering running style.**

The trotting style of the sprinter is not choppy or stilted, but not long and flowing either. The **trotting style is moderate**. Thus, trotting—dogs with the sprinting drivetrain—move their feet faster at a given stride length than dogs built for sustained trotting. The same dog pictured below sprinting around the flock.

A dog with a sound, balanced trot should translate into the ability to outmaneuver livestock and travel all day.

An example of a dog pivoting off the centerline to change directions.

3 Dog Architecture

Anatomical Terminology

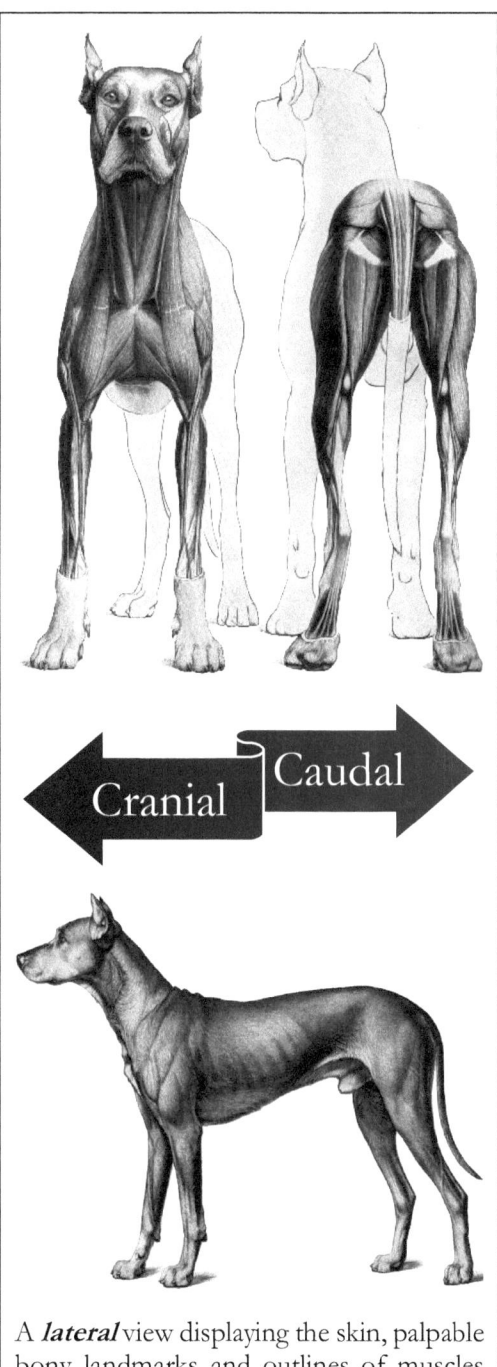

A *lateral* view displaying the skin, palpable bony landmarks and outlines of muscles are easily seen in short coated dogs.

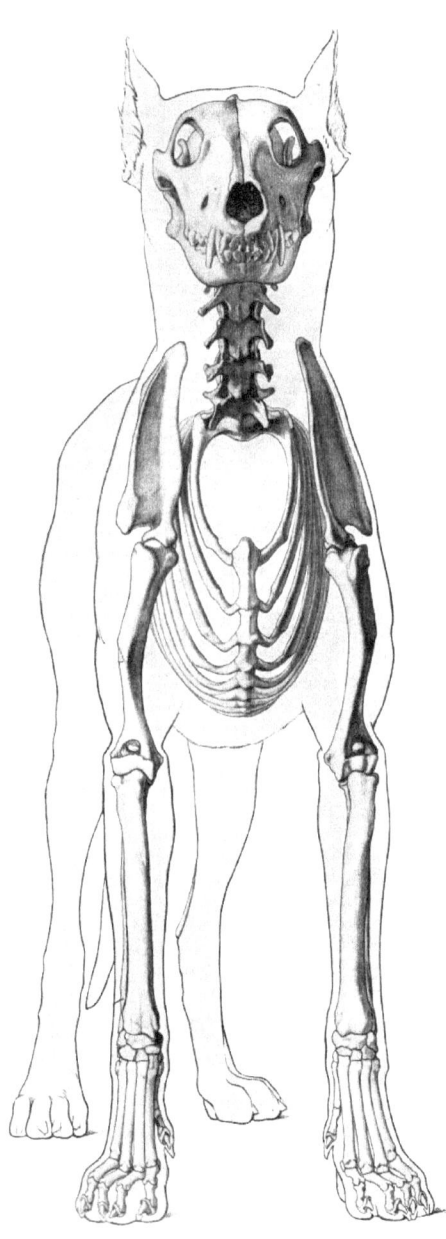

Virtually all breeds of dogs have the same number of bones in their skeleton. Exceptions are dogs without tails, longer tails, and the polydactyl Norwegian Lundehund. They are also tied together by the same quantity of muscles, tendons and ligaments.

Before we get into the architecture of the dog, it is necessary to learn some useful terms for describing body structure. Anatomical terminology has been developed to mark the position of various body parts.

Here's a standard list of anatomical vocabulary:

Anterior: From Latin *anterior*, forward. Front side of the body: chest, abdomen, knees. For instance, the patella is located on the anterior side of the stifle. The toes are anterior to the foot.

Caudal: From Latin *cauda*, meaning "tail." It's used to describe the rear (hind) portion of the dog. The caudal vertebrae are in the tail end of the spinal column.

Cranial: Related to the head. From Latin *crania*, skeleton of the head. Front portion of the dog, toward the head.

Deep: From English terminology, refers to something farther away from the surface, and closer to the center of the body, such as the difference between the deep pectoral muscle, and the superficial pectoral muscle, which lies near the outer surface.

Distal: Structures or part of the limb that lies farther away from the main part of the dog's body or point of attachment. For example, the dog's foot is the most distal part of the leg.

Dorsal: Toward the spine or topline, and corresponding surface of the head, neck and tail.

Dorsal plane: The dorsal plane divides the dog into ventral and dorsal portions. It's analogous to the frontal or coronal plane in humans and runs parallel to the back and the corresponding surfaces of the head, neck, and tail. For example, dolphins and sharks are identified by their dorsal fins.

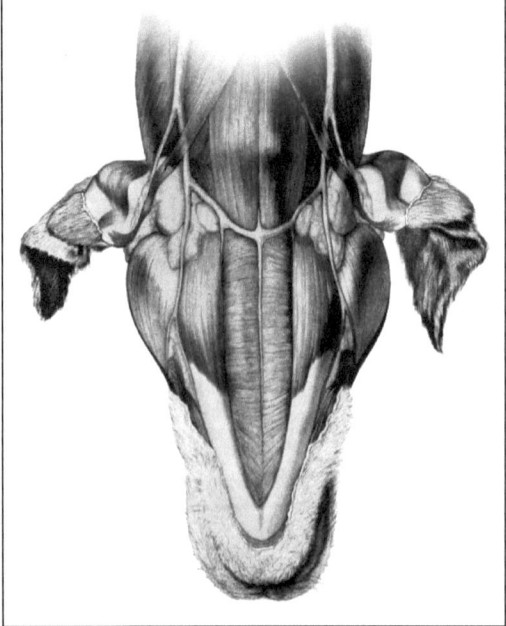

Above: A ***dorsal*** view showing the superficial muscles of the head. **Below:** A ***ventral*** view of the head displaying muscles, vessels, and glands.

Lateral: Toward the side of the body. Away from the central or midline of the dog's body. Also refers to the outside or external part of a surface. For example, the paw's furthermost lateral digital pad contacts the ground first, then the foot rotates medially (inward).

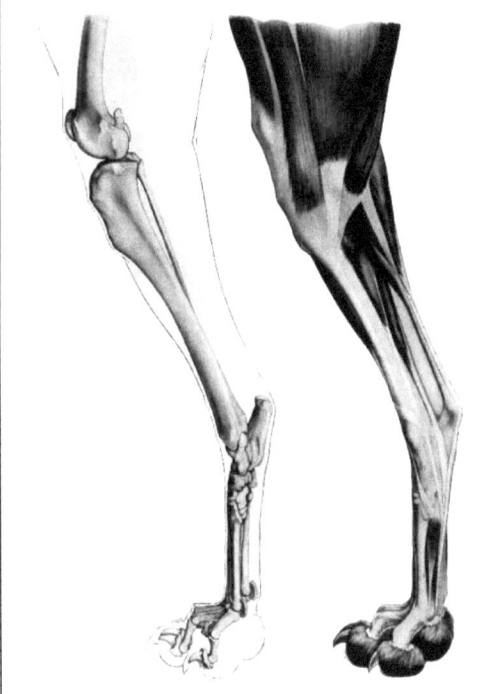

Above: a *medial* view of the bones and muscles of the dog's lower or distal hindlimb from the stifle to the ground.

Medial: From Latin *medius*, structures that lie toward the midline (median plane). Also refers to an inner or more internal part.

Median plane: Midline of the body. It divides the body into symmetrical right and left halves (head, neck, trunk, tail).

Palmer: The bottom surface of the thoracic (forelimb) below the carpus that bears the footpads and the dewclaw; the opposite surface (e.g. the front surface of the paw).

Above: A *dorsal* view of the forefoot illustrating tendons and ligaments. **Below:** *Palmer* view of the forefoot showing various tendons and the carpal pad.

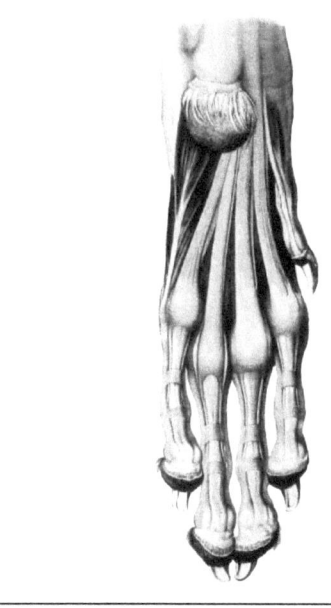

Plantar: The bottom surface of the paw of the pelvic (hindlimb) below the tarsal joint that bears the footpads.

Posterior: Farther back in position; of or nearer the rear or caudal end of the body. The dog's molars, for example, are located in the posterior region of the jaw.

Proximal: Used to describe parts of the limb that lie near or closer to the dog's trunk or point of attachment. For example, the top of the limb that attaches to the body, such as the shoulder.

Rostral: Rostral is used to describe the position of structures within the head toward the end of the dog's nose.

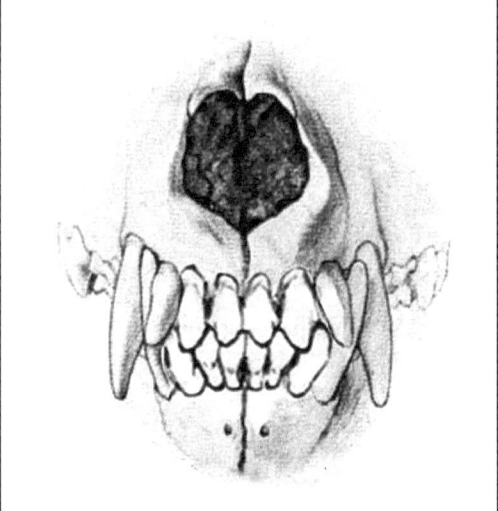

A *rostral* view of the skull highlighting the teeth, specifically the incisors and canines.

Sagittal plane: It divides the dog's body into left and right halves (head, neck, trunk, tail). The sagittal plane runs parallel to the median plane, but not directly along the dog's centerline.

Superficial: From Latin meaning surface. Toward the body's surface. Also called external. For instance, the superficial fascia, immediately underlies the three major layers of the skin. Or, the superficial muscles (and underlying deeper ones) are attached to the bones.

Transverse plane (or cross section): Divides the body into cranial and caudal portions. It runs perpendicular to the long axis of the body (head, neck, trunk, tail) or a limb.

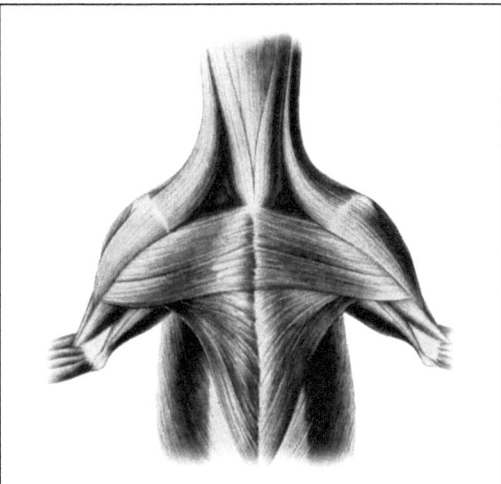

A *ventral* (belly side) view exposing the superficial muscles of the *caudal* neck, proximal forelimb and thoracic regions.

Ventral: From Latin *venter*, meaning "belly." It refers to the underside of the body and corresponding surfaces of the head, neck, and tail.

Skeleton

The dog's skeleton provides the internal framework of the body. Skeletal muscles are attached to the bones, and internal organs are found in the cavities surrounded by the bones and skeletal muscles.

The skeletal system protects the soft tissues. Bones are the hard, rigid form of connective tissue, but they are not lifeless structures. Within their framework are countless living bone cells. They also contain red bone marrow, a soft form of connective tissue, that is the blood cell forming tissue that produces both red and white blood cells.

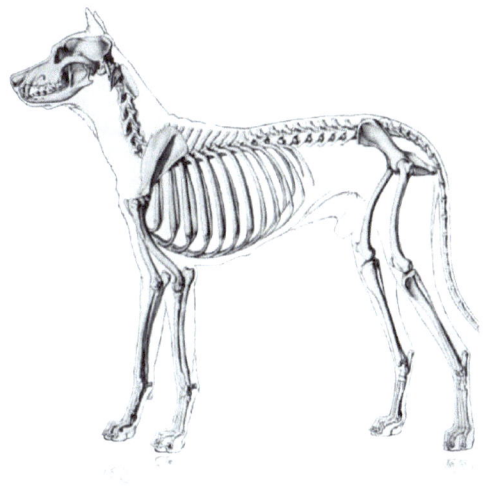

There are five types of bones:

1. **Long bones:** humerus, tibia
2. **Short bones:** carpals and tarsals
3. **Flat bones:** ribs, scapula, sternum
4. **Irregular bones:** vertebrae
5. **Sesamoids:** patella

The bones of the skeletal system contain two major types of connective tissue: bone and cartilage. Cartilage both resembles and differs from bone. Collagenous fibers reinforce the matrix of both tissues. However, in cartilage the fibers are embedded in a firm gel instead of a calcified cement substance like they are in bone. As a result, cartilage has the flexibility of a firm plastic rather than the rigidity of bone. It provides a smooth surface so the bones can move with minimal friction. Cartilage also cushions joint ends to absorb jolts.

Articulations, commonly known as joints, are formed when two bones are joined together. Every bone in the dog's body except one (hyoid bone in the neck that anchors the tongue), connects to at least one other bone. Joints hold the bones together securely and at the same time make it possible for movement to occur between the bones. They can be fixed, slightly movable, or freely movable.

There are two types of moveable joints: amphiarthroses and diarthroses, as compared to a non-moveable joint known as synarthroses, as would be seen in maxio-nasal or internasal sutures on the skull, for example.

Amphiarthroses are joints with slight flexibility. They are usually made up of cartilage, which joins the bones tightly, but frequently with slight movement.

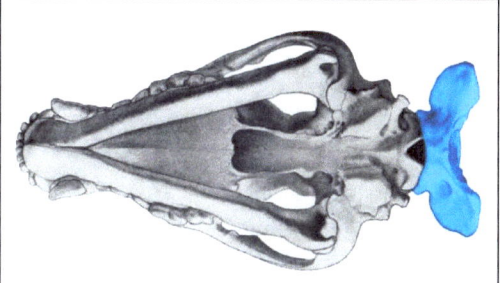

Ventral view of the atlas, the first cervical vertebra (C1), and a diarthrosis joint.

Diarthroses are the freely moveable joints. They have a joint capsule, a joint cavity, and a layer of articular cartilage at the ends of two joining bones. The joint capsule is constructed of tough fibrous connective tissue – and is coated with smooth, slippery synovial lining.

Diarthroses joints include:

1. **Ball and socket joints** e.g., shoulder and hip joints
2. **Condyloid joints** e.g., base of fingers, and wrist
3. **Gliding joints** e.g., vertebrae
4. **Hinge joints** e.g., elbow, knee, hip joints
5. **Pivot joints** e.g., atlas (page 19)

Hinge joints, similar to hinges on a door, allow two directional movements, bending (flexion) and straightening (extension).

Pivot joints, the projection of the axis, the second cervical vertebra (C2) is a point around which an arch of the atlas can pivot. This enables rotation of the head, which rests on the atlas.

Ligaments

Ligaments are the flexible structures that bind together the musculoskeletal system. Ligaments connect bones to bones. They are interwoven in a crisscross pattern like the fibers of a rope. They stabilize legs, for example, by holding the small bones in the knee together. They also will wrap around other joints, keeping them tight and allowing very little motion except in the intended direction.

The vertebrae of the spine are held together by very thick supraspinous ligaments. Ligaments are cords or bands made of the same strong fibrous connective tissue as the joint capsule that connects bones or cartilage to support and strengthen joints. They also grow out of the periosteum and articulate the two bones together even more firmly.

There's little stretch available in ligaments, but they do help to absorb some of the shock and other forces that come from twisting, turning, and bending.

Tendons

Tendons attach muscles to bones and transfer muscular forces by pushing and pulling the bones. They are longer and more flexible than ligaments and can take the form of fibrous cords of dense connective tissue that extends from the fascicles or muscle coverings.

Fascia

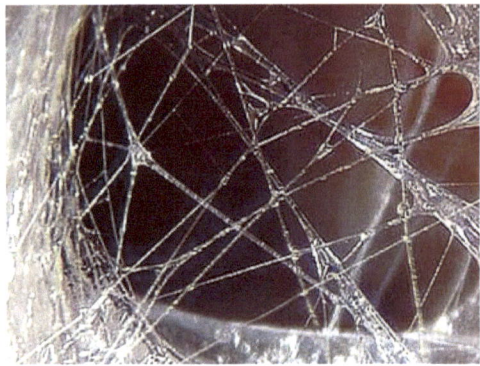

Fascia provides continuity of the muscle-tendon-bone unit. It's the living matrix like a spider web of elastic tissue that surrounds and supports every structure of the dog's body from the surface of the skin to the nucleus of the cell and brings it all together.

Posture and mobility depend on fascia. It's pure collagen. The molecule that makes up fascia is helical or spiral, which is why it always returns to its original shape and why it stores kinetic energy.

Another component to fascia is hyaluronic acid, also known as hyaluronan. Its main function is to retain water (up to 1000 times its weight) to keep connective tissues well lubricated and moist. Hyaluronic acid allows smooth gliding between tendons and adjacent structures.

Muscles

There are two types of muscles in the dog's body, smooth (involuntary) and striated skeletal (voluntary). All muscles are made up of two types of tissue: muscle tissue and connective tissue. Muscles generate force and the highly tensile connective tissue transmits the energy.

Smooth Muscles

The cardiac muscle is highly specialized and is only found in the heart. It's striped with branching fibers that interconnect and allow the heart to act as a unit. It has powerful contractions that are capable of capable of rapid changes of speed.

The remaining smooth or visceral muscles line the body cavities, blood vessels, digestive tract, bladder, and uterus. There are no striations and the cells are spindle-shaped with a central nucleus. Working automatically, they have a slower contraction time than skeletal muscles, but can maintain rhythmic contractions for long periods, which allows progressive wavelike contractions of the hollow tubes of the body, esophagus, stomach, and intestines.

Skeletal Muscles

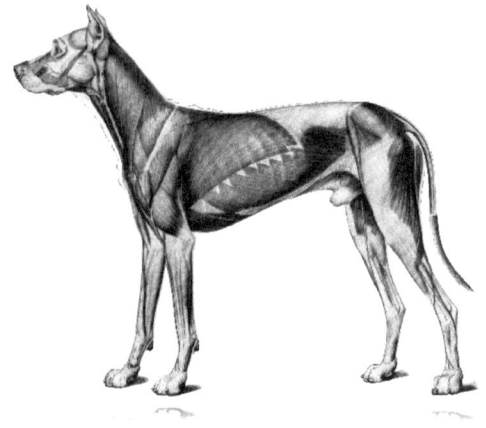

Skeletal muscles are organs composed mainly of skeletal muscle fibers and connective tissue. Every muscle from superficial to deep, or more simply put, outside to the inside, is wrapped in a sleeve of fascia. Normal muscle function depends on the fascial system. A certain amount of force generated by muscle is due to its surrounding fascia.

Muscle Function

The cellular level of musculature is reflected in the muscle fibers. Skeletal muscle is a genetically determined mixture of both Type 1 (slow-twitch) and Type 2 (fast-twitch) fiber types. Each of these muscle types are ideally suited for particular types of activities. The fast twitch fibers produce a lot of power in a short amount of time. In contrast, slow twitch fibers are able to generate less power, but can sustain it for long periods of time. To do this, they require large amounts of oxygen and mitochondria, the organelles that use oxygen to help create ATP (adenosine triphosphate) in order to meet the demands of sustained muscle contractions.

Overall, the forelimb muscles contain a higher proportion of Type I fibers than those of the hindlimbs. These muscle fibers use oxidative pathways to produce energy (pathways that require oxygen). Sometimes they are called red fibers because they contain large amounts of myoglobin, a protein, which can bind and store oxygen. They also have more mitochondria for generating energy aerobically.

The second group of muscle fibers are fast-twitch muscles. They are called "white fibers" because they contain significantly less oxygen due to their lower level of myoglobin. Fast-twitch muscles are divided into two different types: 2A, which is referred to as **fast-twitch oxidative glycolytic** because they use oxygen to help convert glycogen to ATP, and 2B **fast-twitch glycolytic**, which rely on ATP stored in the muscle cells to generate energy. They have a high threshold and will be activated when the force demands are greater than the slow-twitch fibers can meet.

Fast-twitch muscle fibers take a shorter time to reach peak force and can generate more force than slow-twitch ones, such as for powerful, explosive bursts of movement like sprinting.

The distribution of red and white muscle fiber types fluctuate from one muscle to another muscle. They differ in their nerve supply, also. The density of oxidative fibers increases toward the bone.

One uniqueness dogs enjoy compared to other animals is their lack of purely glycolytic type IIB fibers. Dogs have a mixed fiber type known as type IIA/X or IIX for short. These muscle fibers are located in their legs. Type IIX contain a numerous supply of capillaries. Capillaries carry blood away from the body and exchange nutrients, waste, and oxygen with tissues at the cellular level. The extraordinary stamina dogs possess is attributed to Type IIX fibers. Dogs, unlike most all other mammals, can keep all their muscle fibers working over long periods. This is primarily due to the unique composition of their oxygen efficient muscles. Muscle efficiency reduces the danger of muscle over-acidification. Acidity is what causes muscles to become fatigued.

Researchers have found that myostatin mutations are associated with increased muscling, distribution of fast-twitch muscle fibers, and hindquarter power. The ratio of fast-twitch to slow-twitch fibers is one of the main reasons some dogs excel in performance events.

Variations in the myostatin (MSTN) gene, a muscle protein, is associated with skeletal muscle fiber composition in a range of mammalian species including the dog. It's also linked to sprinting ability.

Research has indicated racing Whippets that carried one copy of the mutated gene were among the fastest runners, but those that carried two copies developed bulky, heavy muscles caused by a myostatin deficiency.

Skeletal muscles fall into categories depending on their function:

1. **Extensors:** prevent unintended flexion of the joints by isometric contraction
2. **Flexors:** determine the degree that muscles are able to extend
3. **Abductors:** move the bones away from body's midline
4. **Adductors:** move the bones toward the body's midline
5. **Pronators/Supinators:** rotate the bone around its long-axis

Skeletal muscles attach to bone, or sometimes other muscles or tissues, at two or more places. Most of the dog's skeletal muscles attach to two bones with movable joints between them. They are usually demarcated on the basis of their *origin* and *insertion* and the nerves that supply them. The muscle **attaches** to the more stable or stationary bone and is known as the *origin*, such as the dog's masseter muscle that originates from the front part of the zygomatic arch (bridge of bone connecting face and cranium below the eye). It inserts on the mandible and is called the muscle's *insertion* point. The insertion moves toward the origin. So, in the case of the masseter muscle it raises the mandible to close the mouth. Joint movements are therefore controlled by cooperative antagonism of muscles. In this book I often use the word **attachment** rather than insertion to make it simpler and easier to understand.

Each dog has about 350 pairs of muscles. I won't list each and every one, since it's not the purpose of this book. There are some good anatomy books, pictorial and otherwise, that will give you a much more complete look at muscles and their function.

That said, it's useful to be familiar with the major muscles or muscle groups and how they work. Muscles within a group tend to have similar actions. Some muscles perform functions at more than one joint. Additionally, internal muscles that lie beneath the external ones all work together in harmony. It's also helpful to know muscles are named in Latin or English for their function or structure and/or location.

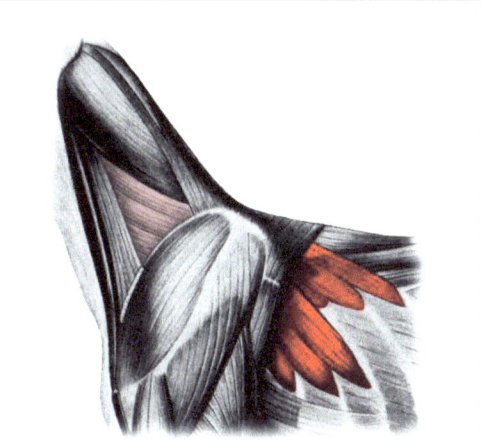

The serratus ventralis originates from the ribs and inserts into the shoulder blade under the scapula. The cervical portion is pictured in pink / thoracic portion in red.

For instance, the thoracic portion of the serratus ventralis, a large fan-shaped muscle which originates from the ribs (pictured above) is responsible for suspending the canine trunk. The pectoral and rhomboideus muscles are responsible for stabilizing the pivot point of the shoulder blade and for protraction and retraction of the forelimbs.

Here's a quick look at a few of the dog's muscles and muscle groups (not listed in alphabetical order):

Abdominal Obliques

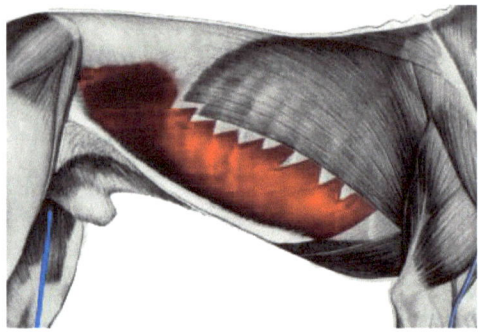

The abdominal muscles are the abs or obliques. This is the area humans refer to as the "six-pack." They are respectively the deep aponeurosis, the sheet of pearly white fibrous tissue that takes the place of a tendon in flat muscles having a wide area of attachment. The superficial abs are found between the ribs. They assist in the breathing process as well as protect and support the weight of the internal organs.

Latissimus Dorsi

The latissimus dorsi is Latin for "broadest" and "dorsum" for back. "Lats", as they are often referred to, belong to the superficial layer of back muscles.

Not only are the limbs important for locomotion, but the back musculature is as well. Research conducted by zoologists at the Friedrich-Schiller-Universität Jena Germany discovered the dog's lats don't engage when the dog is running horizontally, but are activated when running against gravity, such as racing up an A-frame in Agility, while towing a sled or when leash pulling.

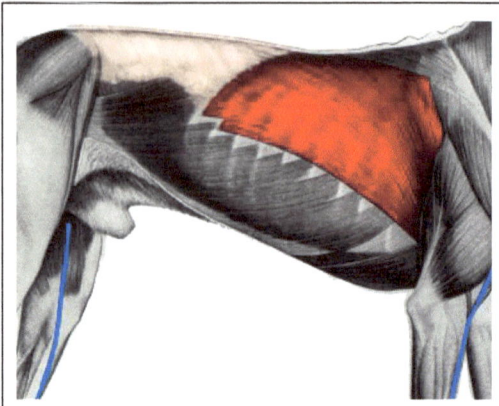

The latissimus dorsi pictured with the lumbo-dorsal fascia (pinkish-beige).

Rhomboideus

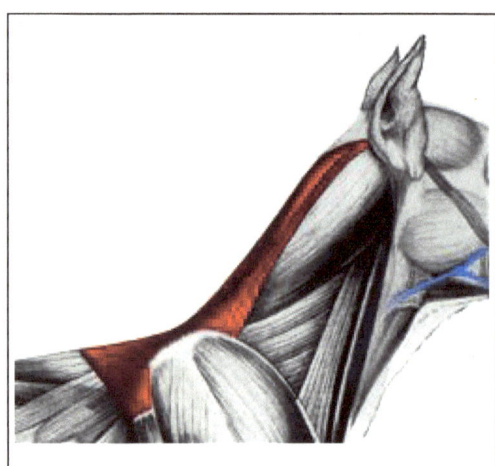

The cervical rhomboid muscle

The cervical rhomboid muscle originates from the spinatuscervical vertebrae. They are underneath the trapezius muscles and not visible from the outside. These muscles can't be seen, but they are responsible for stabilizing the pivot point of the scapula and for the protraction and retraction of the forelimbs.

Brachiocephalic

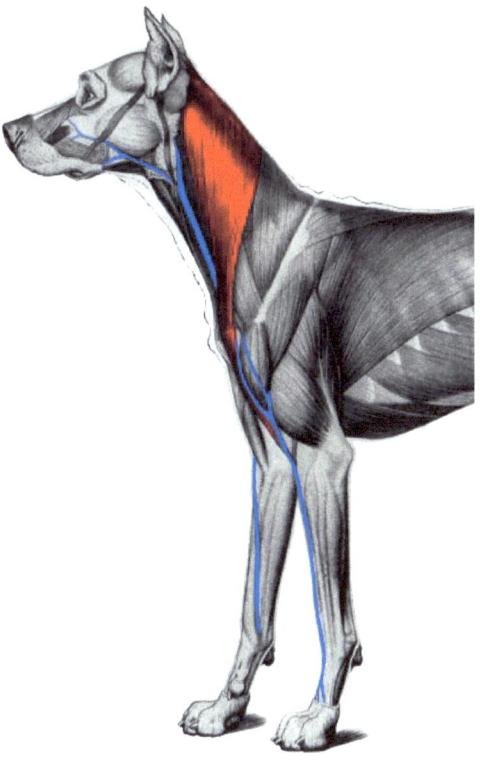

The brachiocephalic muscle on the neck is considered the main shoulder extensor and protractor of the forelimb during the swing phase. It moves the head and neck to either side and brings the shoulder and forelimbs forward. It lengthens the neck to extend, such as when the dog is jumping or low-heeling a cow. The use of a tight leash restricts the movement of this muscle, which can cause gaiting faults in the conformation show ring. Certainly, you've heard judges say, "Take them around on a loose leash."

Trapezius

The trapezius, a diamond-shaped quadrilateral, is located at the base of the neck between either side of the withers and over the rhomboideus and splenius muscles. The main function of the trapezius muscle is to stabilize the pivot point of the scapula.

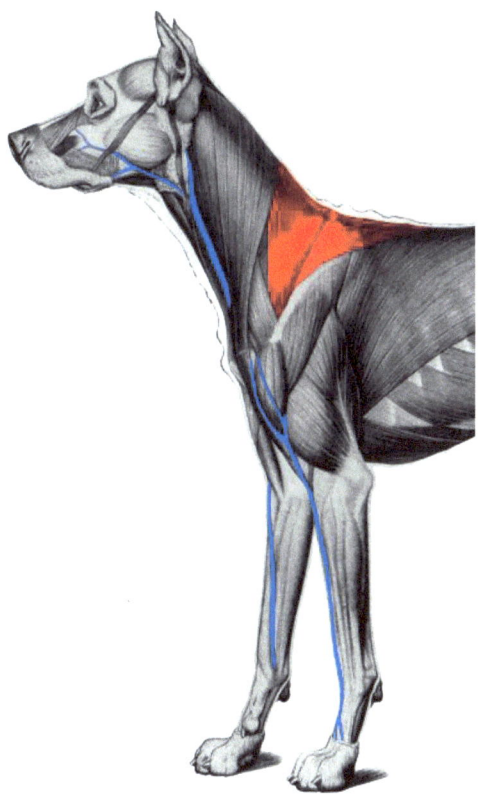

In humans, the trapezius muscles help elevate the shoulders and help to extend the neck backward. But in dogs these are anti-gravity muscles that help counterbalance when dogs move across uneven terrain.

Pectorals

The main muscle group of the chest are the pectorals. They are divided into two parts, the deep or pectoralis major, and the superficial or pectoralis minor. The thick muscle fibers of the deep pectoral muscle attach to the dog's sternum, the costal cartilages, and the xiphoid cartilage, and insert inside the humerus.

The pectorals are the adductor muscles of the forelimb. They support retraction of the limbs and prepare for takeoff. They move the body over the supporting foreleg during the stance phase, as well as extend the shoulder and pull the humerus back.

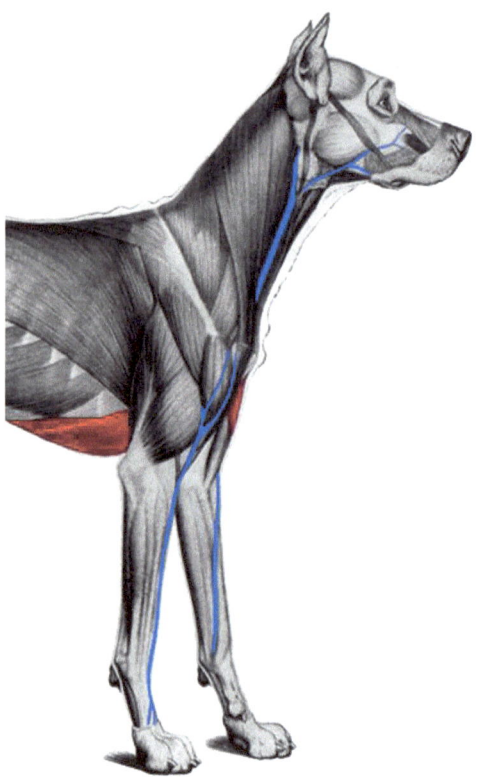

The superficial pectoral, which is attached to the prosternum and to the top of humerus, draws the humerus into the body as well as forward and backward to advance and adduct the leg.

Triceps

Triceps or *triceps brachii*, which is Latin for "three-headed muscle of the arm", is a triangular section that has four heads in dogs, not three. It attaches to the upper arm (humerus) and to the olecranon process (point of the elbow). It forms a muscular protuberance at the lower part of the shoulder, just above the elbow joint.

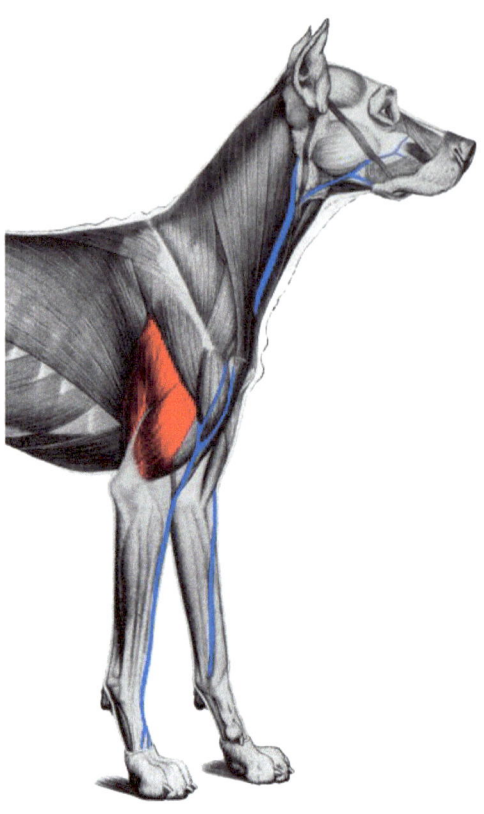

The long head of the triceps is activated at the beginning of the stance phase. It's an antigravity muscle that helps stabilize the thoracic limbs. It becomes an extensor when the dog is laying on its back stretching its legs.

Deltoids

The deltoid muscle group along with the infraspinatus support the shoulder laterally and can extend, flex and stabilize the shoulder joint during the stance phase while the limb is load-bearing. The infraspinatus, an antigravity muscle that stabilizes the thoracic limbs during touchdown. It also helps flex the humeral joint and abduct the limb.

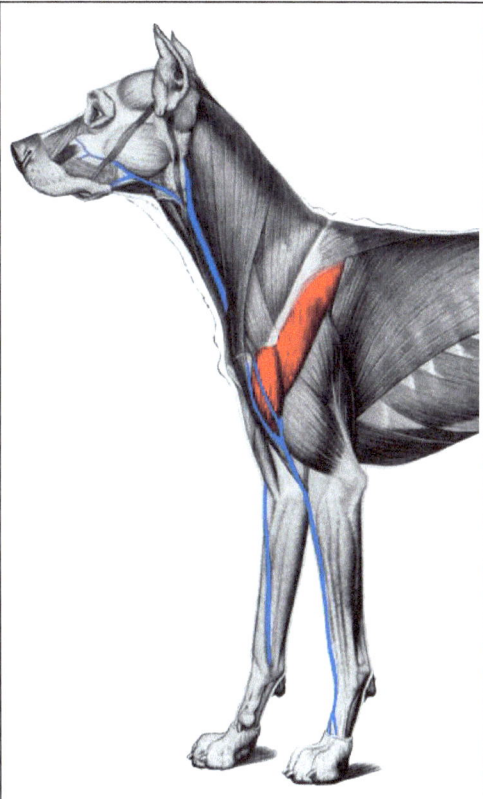

Above: The deltoids. Below: A lateral view of a small portion of the infraspinatus.

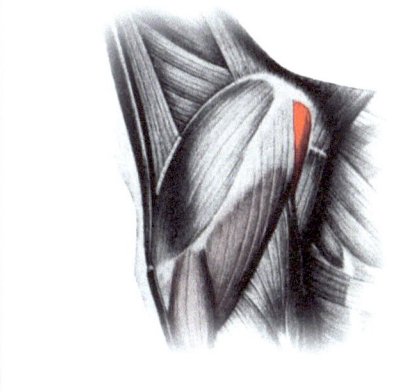

Gluteal

The gluteal group of the rump is the heavily muscled part of the first, or upper thigh, and becomes part of the buttocks. As a group, they are responsible for the extension and rotation of the hip, hock, and stifle, which generate forward thrust and ability to jump.

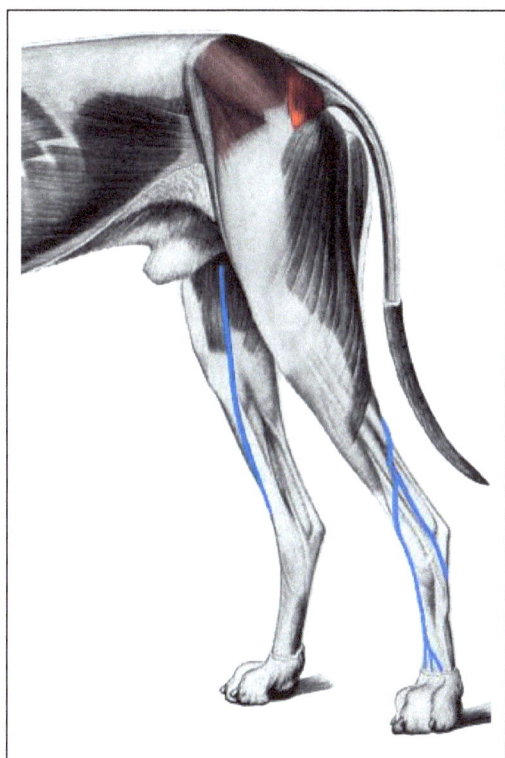

The superficial gluteal muscle lies caudal to the middle gluteal muscle.

Hamstrings

The hamstrings cover the upper thigh and attach to the stifle. They cross the hip and stifle. Its main function during the stance phase is for antigravity. During locomotion the hamstring muscles are responsible for retraction and propulsion of the body. The biceps femoris (pictured on 28) is the largest muscle in the muscle group. It is superficial and is covered by skin and fascia attaches at the cranial portion of the femur. It flexes the stifle and extends the hock joint at the beginning of the swing phase in locomotion.

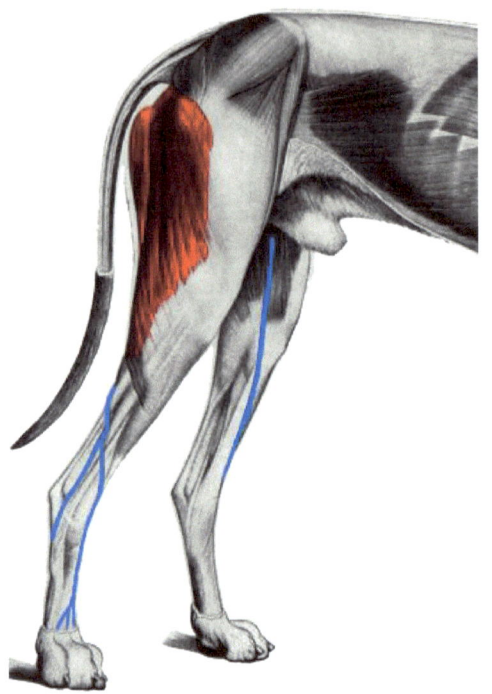

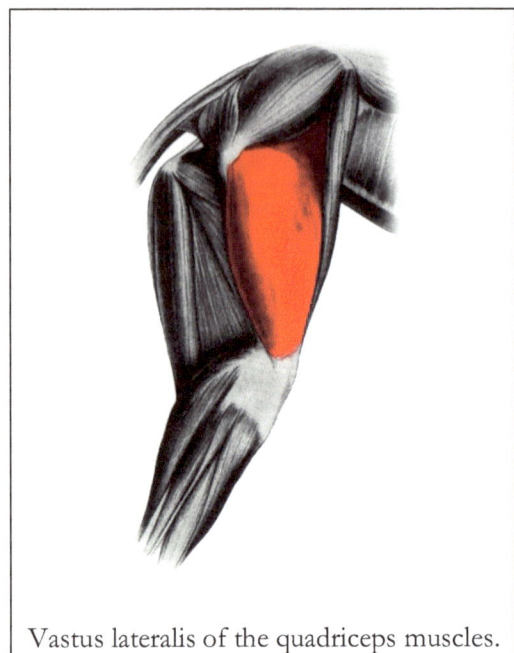

Vastus lateralis of the quadriceps muscles.

When the hamstring muscles flex the stifle during the swing phase, meaning the foot is in the air, their antagonists, the quadriceps group, relax and constrain extension during the first half of the stance phase.

Quadriceps

The quadriceps femoris muscle group is made up of four muscles, hence quads. The four muscles are specifically, vastus lateralis, vastus medius, vastus intermedius, and rectus femoris. They are located at the front part of the upper thigh. The knee joint is held in position by the vastus muscles. The quadriceps are the key antigravity muscles of the pelvic limb and forward motion. They stabilize the stifle against the flexion during the stance phase of motion.

Extensor Muscles of the Carpus and Digits

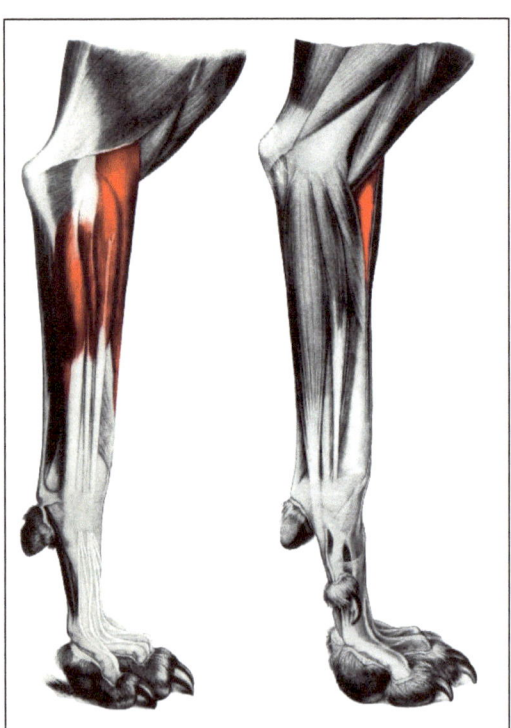

Lateral and medial views of the *extensor* muscles of the forearm.

The extensors originate at the elbows and terminate as tendons in the digits. They regulate the degree of flexion by preventing unintentional bending in the joints. The extensor muscles of the carpi along with the flexors of the carpi are active from touchdown until the middle of the stance phase.

The Flexor Muscles of the Carpus and Digits

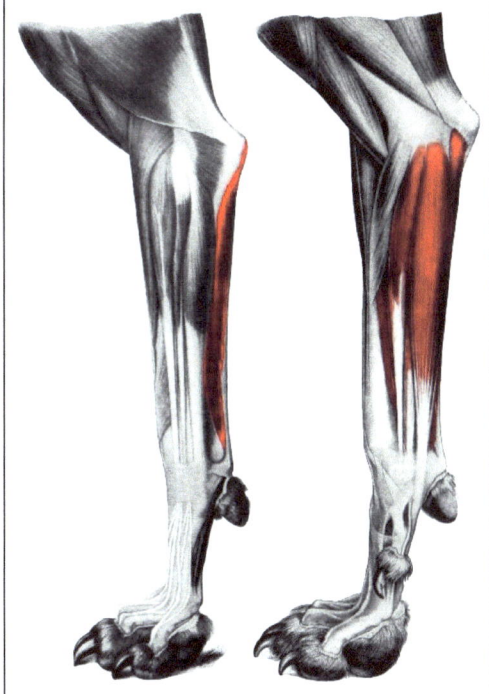

Lateral and medial views of the *flexor* muscle group.

The flexor muscles aid carpal flexion and rotation. They originate at the elbow and conclude as tendons in the digits. They run along the forelimb to the pastern and toes. The flexors are larger and more powerful than the extensors. The main function of the digital flexor muscles and tendons are to flex the digits. They are important for support of the carpal and metacarpophalangeal joints and for sinking the claws into the ground for stable footing. They provide the power to turn the front feet outwards shortly after takeoff. Before touchdown, the paw rotates inward in slight supination and usually touches down pointing inward with the outer edge first and then elevates, lowers, and bends the pastern (carpal joints) and flexes the toes.

The digital flexor muscles and tendons serve other functions as well. They work as a shock absorber when the foot hits the ground, which limits the potential damage to muscles. This system also prevents hyperextension and helps maintain the proper structure of the paws by working to bring the bend back into the toes after the foot is flattened by weight bearing movement.

Self-Test your knowledge on the main muscle groups by labeling the muscle groups on pages 30 – 31 from the word box below:

Muscle groups:

☐ Abdominals
☐ Brachiocephalic
☐ Deltoids
☐ Extensor muscles of the carpus
☐ Flexor muscles of the carpus
☐ Gluteal
☐ Hamstrings
☐ Latissimus dorsi
☐ Masseter Muscle
☐ Pectorals
☐ Trapezius
☐ Triceps

See page 32 for the answers.

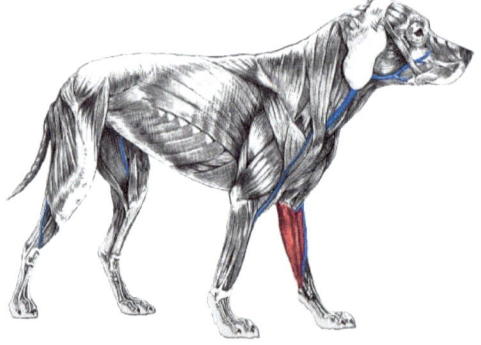

1. _____

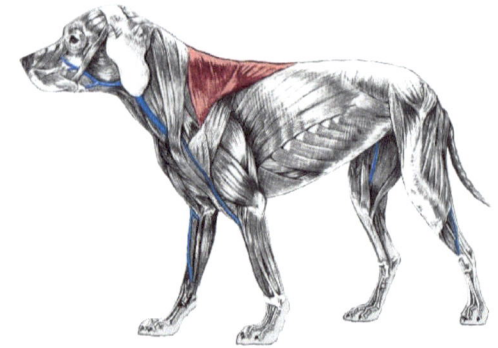

4. _____

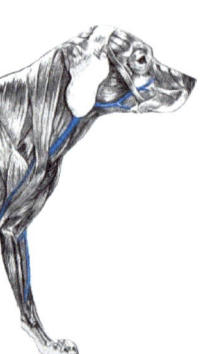

2. _____

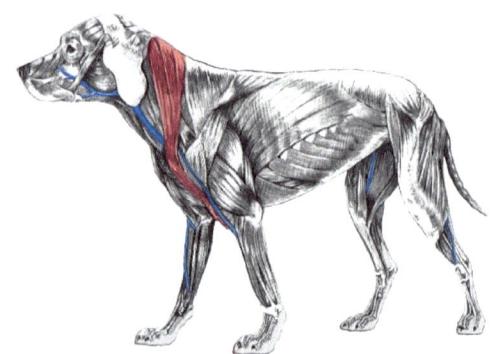

5. _____

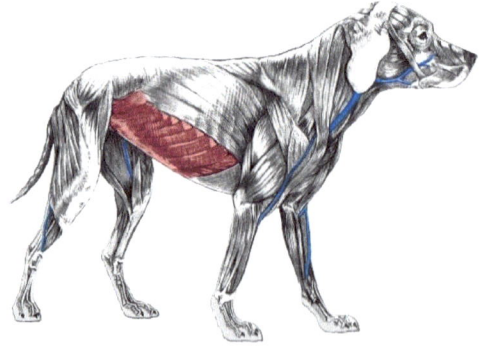

3. _____

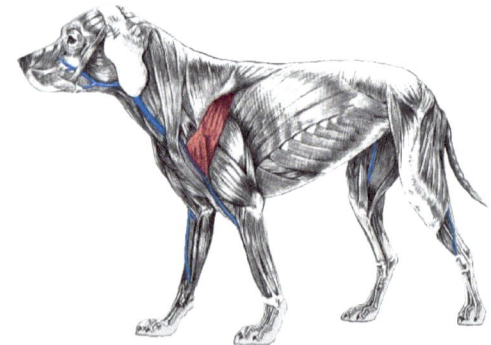

6. _____

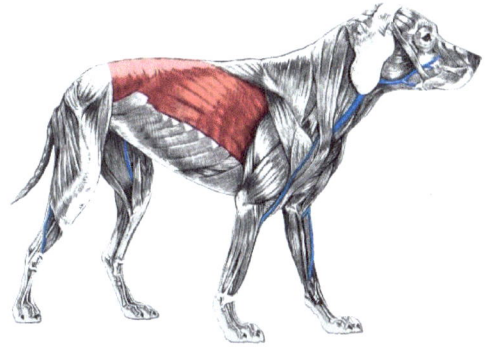
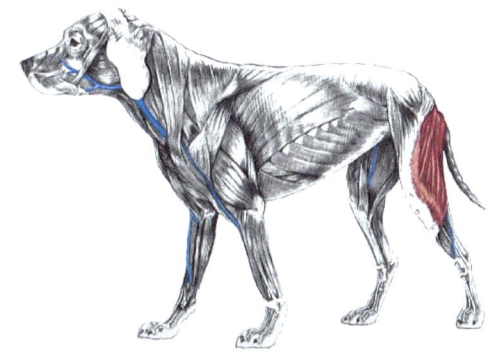

7. _____ 10. _____

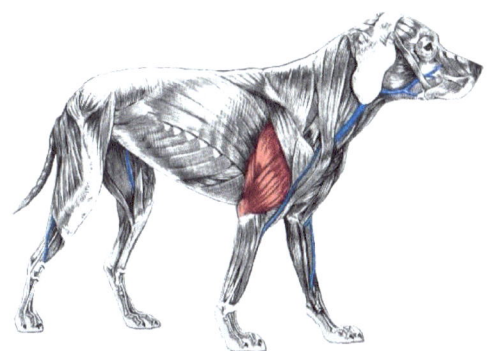
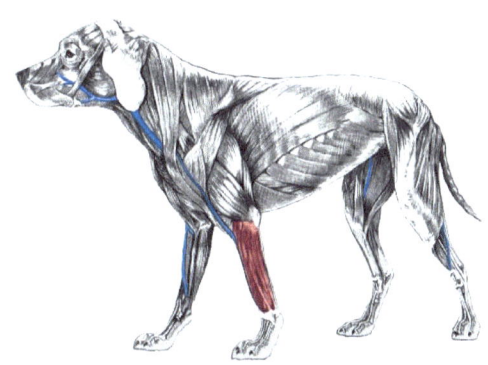

8. _____ 11. _____

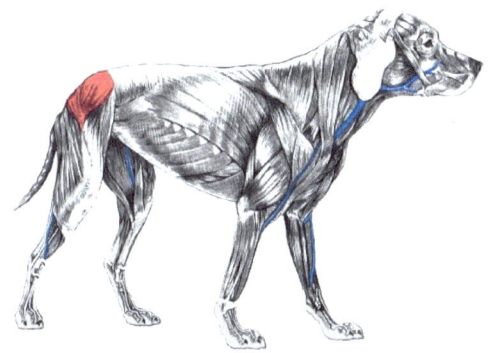
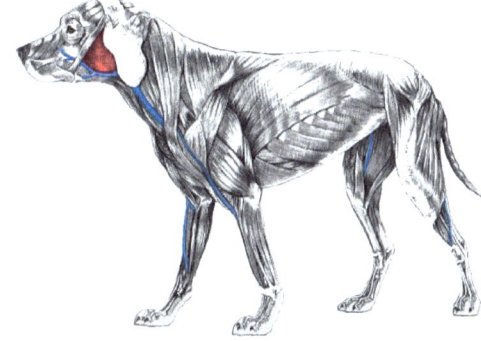

9. _____ 12. _____

Answers:

Abdominals (3)	Hamstrings (10)
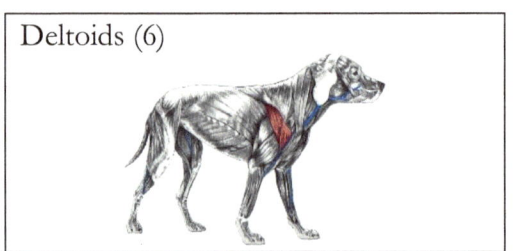	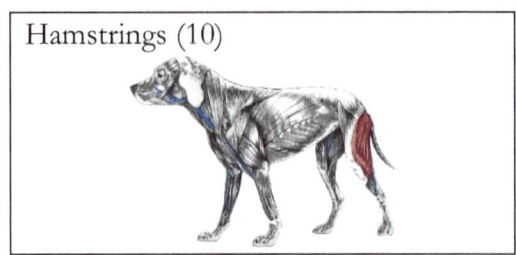

Brachiocephalic (5)	Latissimus Dorsi (7)
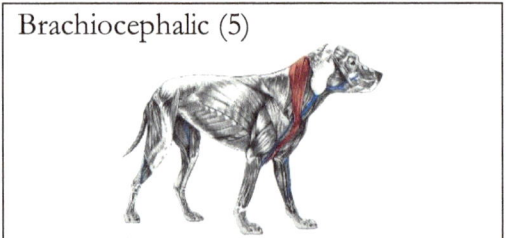	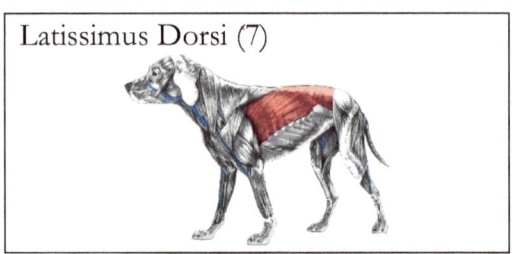

Deltoids (6)	Masseter Muscle (12)
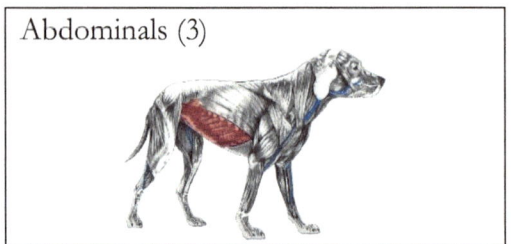	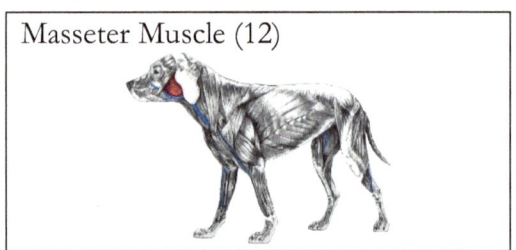

Extensor muscles of the carpus and digits (11)	Pectorals (2)
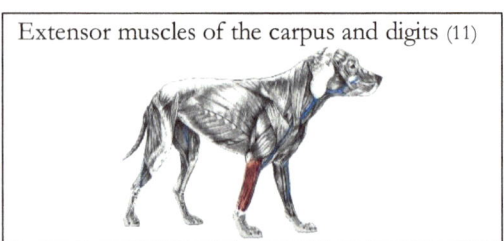	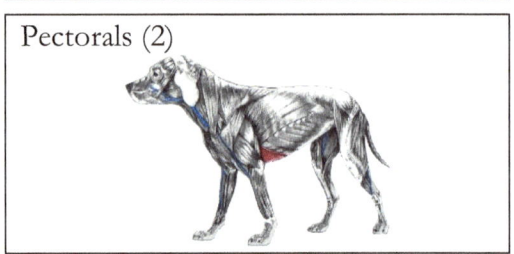

Flexor muscles of the carpus and digits (1)	Trapezius (4)
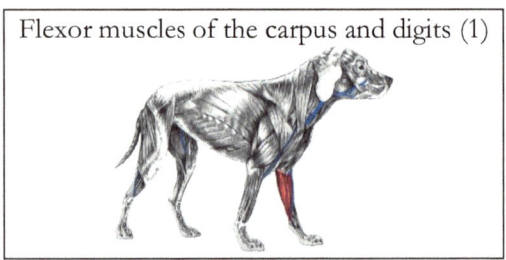	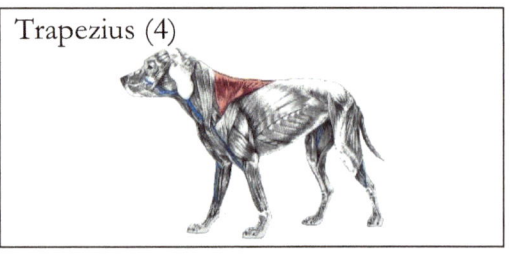

Gluteal (9)	Triceps (8)
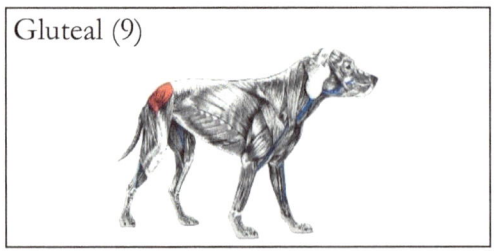	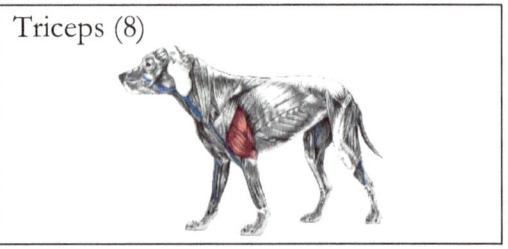

4 Neck, Topline and the Body

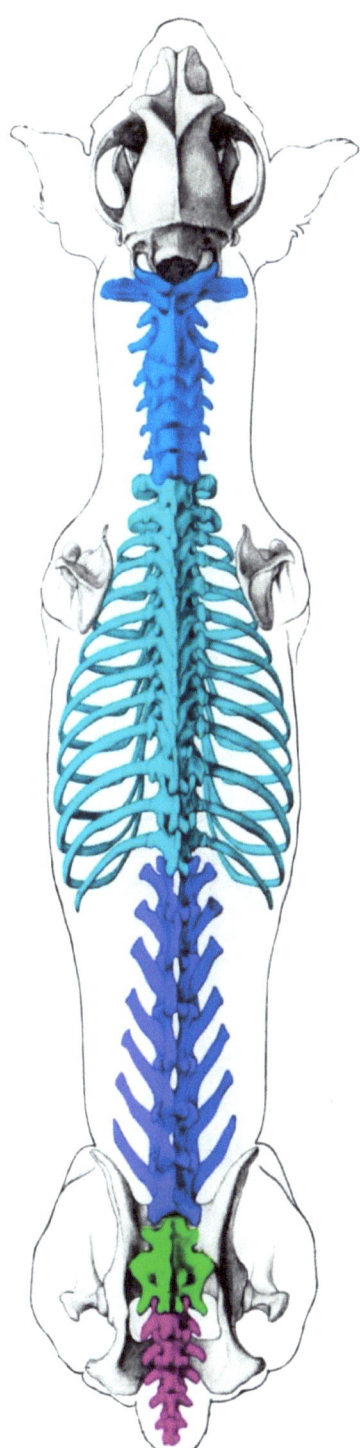

The dorsal view (from above) revealing the bones of the skeleton.

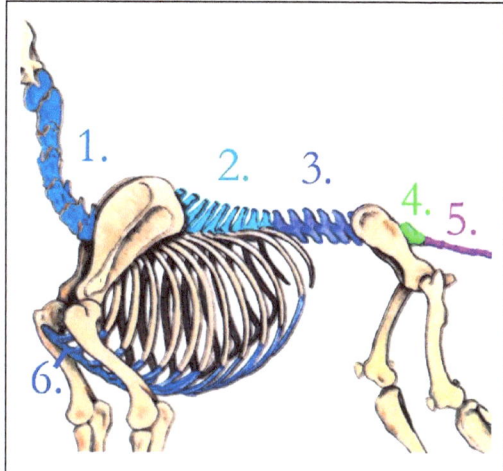

1: Cervical vertebrae (C1 to C7)
2: Thoracic vertebrae (T1 to T13)
3: Lumbar vertebrae (L-1 to l-7)
4: Sacrum
5: Caudal or coccygeal vertebrae
6: Sternum and Costal cartilages that connect the ribs to the sternum and enable the chest cavity to expand for breathing.

The vertebral column can be divided into three segments:

1. Cervical (blue).
2. Thoracic (cyan).
3. Lumbar (purple).

The dog's neck is made up of seven cervical vertebrae (C-1 to C-7 pictured in blue). The next 13 thoracic vertebrae (T-1 to T-13 pictured in cyan) connect to 12 pairs of ribs that support the chest and abdominal region. They are then attached to the sternum on the underside of the chest via a section of cartilage. Additionally, dogs have one pair of floating ribs that are unattached at their lower portion.

Seven lumbar vertebrae (L-1 to L-7 pictured in purple) are located in the most flexible area of the dog's back, the loin. They support the dog's lower back and hindquarters.

The sacrum (pictured in green) is made up of three fused vertebrae, followed by a varied number of coccygeal vertebrae (pictured in magenta), the bones that form the tail.

The cervical part of the spine supports the dog's neck and shoulders. The atlas and axis are often discussed separately from the remaining five vertebrae as they are the most superior bones of the vertebral column.

on his shoulders, connects the skull to the spine. It's a ring of bone that supports the entire skull and acts as a pivot, which allows the head to rotate. It is responsible for the up and down motion of the head and neck.

Articulation with the second cervical vertebrae (C2), the **axis**, acts as a pivot around the atlas and enables the side-to-side movement of the head on the neck.

A dog uses its head and neck for balancing factors. They work together in coordination with the propelling hindquarters—assisting in the dog's maneuverability. Taylor's Escalante, an Australian Shepherd, pictured above and below.

Where the head goes, the body follows.

The atlas, named for the Greek mythical god who supported the world

And, again, the same dog working cattle. It's quite natural for a working dog to drop its head and neck while working a trot. As a point of reference see the carriage of his head and neck while jumping (pictured below).

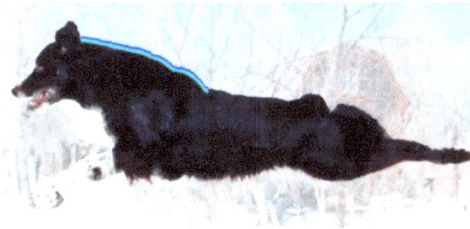

The lift of his neck while jumping perfectly illustrates how the muscles of the neck tie into the shoulders.

In the picture above, a red line between the shoulder blades marks where the trapezius and brachiocephalicus muscles lift from the shoulders to the base of the skull as the dog lunges forward on the ground to heel—nip at the cows to urge them forward.

The brachiocephalicus, a complex muscle that attaches at the base of the skull, travels down the neck and is inserted into the humerus. It is responsible for extending the head and neck or inclining it from one side to the other.

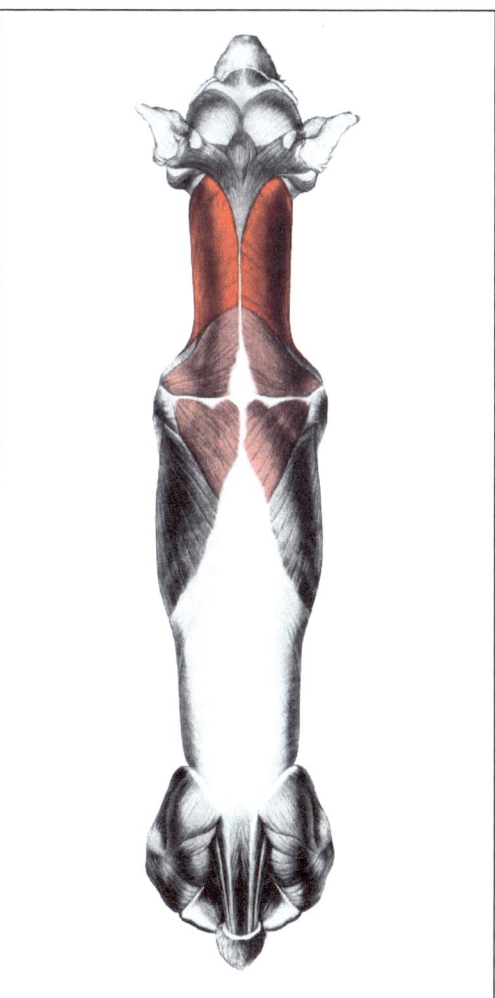

Dorsal view of the brachiocephalicus muscle in bright red cranial to the trapezius muscle in pink.

Separating Fact from Fiction

Do references to a short or long neck mean the vertebrae really are shorter or longer than normal?

The actual length of a dog's neck, regardless if it's short and nestled into the dog's shoulders or long and noticeable, is governed by the relative length of vertebrae and thickness of the cervical discs between adjacent vertebrae that make up the neck. The apparent length depends on the scapula's degree of layback, meaning whether the upper edge of the scapula is upright or oblique.

The dog pictured (above) shows the neck tapering nicely from the head to the shoulders. The upper outline is slightly arched outwards at the crest and merges gradually into the withers.

A strong support from the elastic nuchal-suspraspinous ligament and a well-developed trapezius muscle is desirable to support the weight of the head and neck especially when carrying a small duck or heavier game, such as a goose.

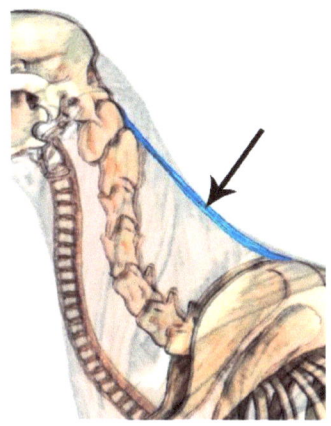

The nuchal ligament is a thick band of highly elastic fibers that stretch and retract. It's responsible for head carriage and stabilizing the base attachments of the muscles that move the thoracic limbs (forelegs) forward and rotate the top of the shoulder blade forward as the foreleg moves backwards. The supraspinous ligament is a continuation of the nuchal ligament. It runs the length of the trunk joining the tips of the vertebrae together.

The ewe neck (shown bottom left column on a horse) is concave. Some people think the ewe neck is caused by inverted cervical vertebrae of the neck. In horses, the ewe neck is linked to poor conditioning and muscle tone. It can affect their ability to flex at the poll.

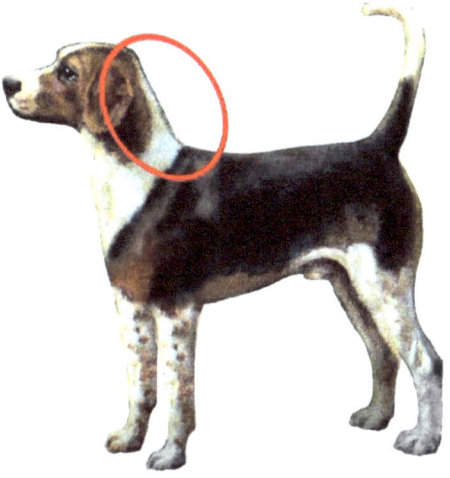

Don't mistake an upright neck for the ewe neck.

Topline

The topline is the "backbone of the operation." The definition of topline, however, can be misleading. Topline is often used in the place of backline.

The topline includes the sloping croup. According to some breed standards, the dog's back is level and firm from the withers to hip joints.

The hip joint is formed where the thigh bone (femur) meets the bones that make up the pelvis. The pelvis is attached to the spinal column by the sacrum.

The back begins at the first and ends at the 13th thoracic vertebrae. The loin begins at the 1st lumbar vertebrae. The vertebrae of the spine are held together by thick supraspinous ligaments. Tendons attach to the collagenous membrane (periosteum) of the bones. Dogs are able to flex and extend the lumbar vertebrae to produce a great deal of power for forward drive.

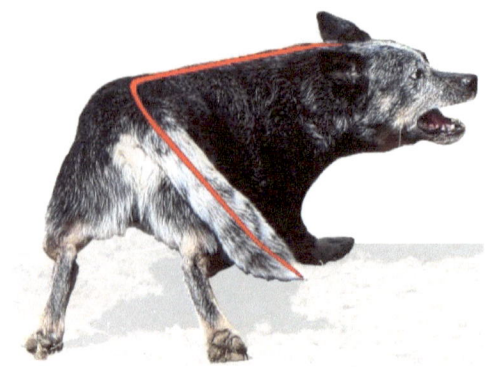

The interwoven group of thoracic and lumbar musculature all support and affect movement. They enable unilateral contraction and flexion (when one side contracts as the other side relaxes). The longissimus dorsi is the longest of the epaxial muscle group and supports nearly every other muscle in the body. The "backstrap" is responsible for stabilizing the trunk as the dog walks and trots. It's the same muscles that give power for forward drive and help deer in its amazing jumping abilities.

You can see the spine twisting from the white tip of the Aussie's bobtail all the way to the tip of its nose as the head turns to grip the cow's heel.

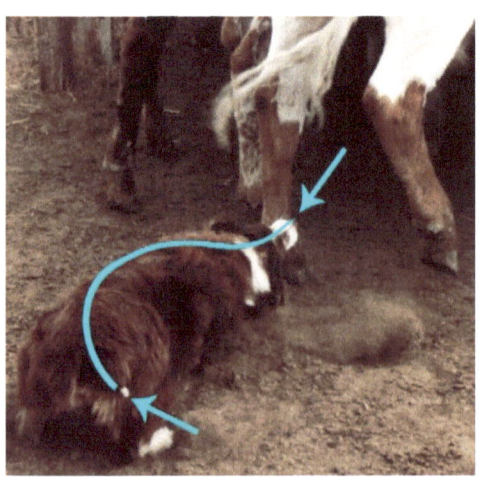

The dorsal-lumbar bow, a small arch (slight rise) over the loin due to muscular development, should not be confused with a roach back. A roach back refers to the convex curvature of thoracic vertebrae, the relatively inflexible section of the back, not the highly flexible lumbar vertebrae of the loin. The Bedlington Terrier breed standard requires a natural arch over the lumbar region because it gives them the same kind of reach that one finds in the Greyhound and the Whippet. The Bedlington was originally bred to hunt vermin and has since been used in dog racing. Its roached back and quick speed stem most likely from its Whippet ancestors. It is not uncommon to see this feature exaggerated by grooming in modern day Bedlington Terriers.

Also, when dogs are physically fit and in working condition, the muscles may be slightly arched over the loin. This is from muscular development, not a curved spine.

The Thorax (Chest)

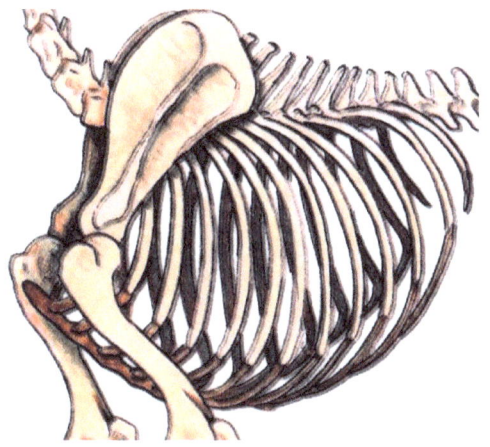

The dog's chest or thorax protects the inner organs—the heart and lungs. It's hung between the shoulders and upper arms and is attached to the limbs by muscles. They include muscles beneath the scapula, extending from the scapula to the cervical and thoracic vertebrae, and to the ribs themselves. The rib cage itself within the forelimbs is capable of a significant degree of movement.

The ribs extend downward from the thoracic vertebrae and connect to the sternum—the lower curved outline of the chest. It's also known as the keel or brisket, which consists of three different bones: the manubrium, the keel, and the xiphoid process. The manubrium of sternum or prosternum is the most forward projection of the rib cage. The bone between the thoracic limbs (the forelegs) is the keel, or brisket, while the rear of the sternum is the xiphoid process.

The xiphoid process is involved in the attachment of many muscles, including the abdominal diaphragm, a layer muscle necessary for normal breathing. It also anchors the abs (rectus abdominis muscles).

Moderate depth, length, and width of the ribs allows adequate chest expansion for breathing, yet tapers effectively to combat lateral displacement (side to side movement) during locomotion like the Bulldog, which has the highest energy consumption of any breed while walking, yet their breathing is handicapped.

Breeds like the Dachshund that were bred to track a burrowing animal into the earth or "go to ground" and squeeze in after it generally have shorter legs. Dogs that go to ground can have chest circumferences or "span" no wider than the animals they hunt.

According to Barry Jones, the founding chairman to the National Working Terriers Federation, "The chest is, without doubt, the determining factor as to whether a terrier may follow its intended quarry underground. Too large and he/she is of little use for underground work, for no matter how determined the terrier may be, this physical setback will not be overcome in the nearly-tight situations it will encounter in working foxes."

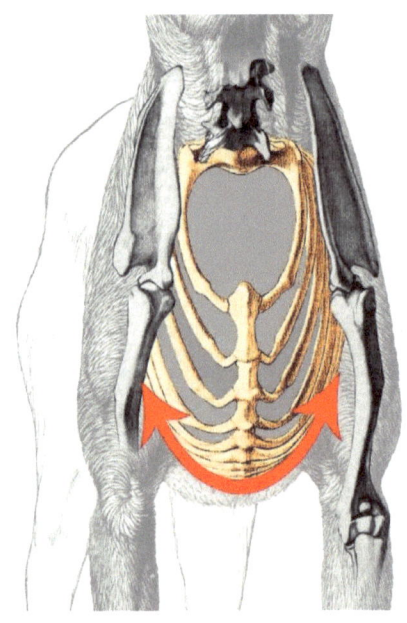

Rib spring refers to the degree of outward curvature of the ribs that form the expandable cage. The first three pairs of ribs are only slightly curved and will gradually increase to the 10th pair. The top of the ribs come out of the thirteen thoracic (chest) vertebrae beginning at the fifth rib.

Thoracic rib spring determines the distance between the forelimbs and influences the action of the forelegs. Rib spring can help or hinder the dog's ability to converge (draw its paws beneath the center of gravity) to minimize lateral displacement (side-to-side motion). Agility is also dependent on convergence, which enables each dog to swivel from the centerline of the body, rather than pulling itself around.

In a natural stance, the dog's forelegs should drop vertically to the ground, not outwards, forming a triangle (narrow at the chest and wide at the base, the feet). It is normal for a young dog to "toe-out" a little. As the dog matures and its chest widens and the pectoral muscles that anchor the inner aspect of the thoracic limbs to the sternum develop, the legs typically line up.

The depth of ribs will not change, but as the young dog develops, the ribs naturally widen outwards causing the elbows to line up correctly.

Any change of the shape of the rib cage, such as a barrel chest or slab-sided or flat ribs, can also affect the dog's gait. Why? Because it directly impacts placement of the upper arm and elbow.

The shape of the wolf's rib cage has been described like the keel or front of a boat that enables the elbows to tuck closely to or just under the rib cage.

Thoracic wall anomalies can vary from mild to severe including pigeon chest (Pectus Carinatum) and barrel chest. Pigeon chest occurs when the costal cartilage, which connects the ribs to the sternum, grows outwards rather than flat along the chest wall pushing the sternum forward. The manubrium comes to a point rather than flush against the chest. It can affect lung and heart function. Some might experience exercise intolerance. There may also be other abnormalities, such as a "herring gut" where the ribcage doesn't go back far enough into the abdomen resulting in a lack of structural support.

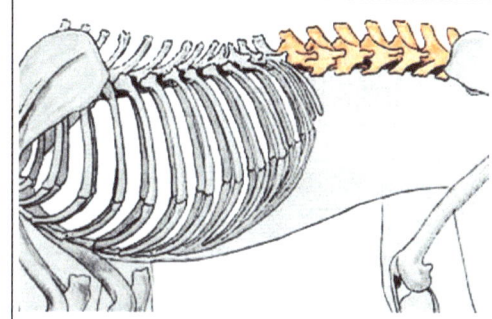

You can see the back ends at the last or 13th thoracic vertebrae and the loin begins at the first lumbar vertebrae (in brown).

The abdomen lies behind the ribs. The abdominal muscles protect and support the abdominal viscera and flex the spinal column.

The bottom line carries well back with an abdominal tuck-up. The incline of the tuck-up is important because it enables the pelvic limbs to fold underneath the body, maneuver and turn sharply. It should begin at the 9th rib. If it tucks up too soon or abruptly, it restricts the heart and lung function and is referred to as a herring gut.

The loin (coupling) refers to the area from the ribs to the pelvis. It's where the body tucks up when the dog sprints or while moving into or out of position to heel a cow or dodge an attack. A healthy lumbar region is necessary for agility.

The loin is flexible because of the absence of ribs. It needs to be muscular (broad when viewed from above) because it's not supported by any other bones of the structure. It contains thick, telegraphic muscles that surround seven lumbar vertebrae and transmits the power from the hindquarter to the shock-absorbing forequarter. In dogs and all other mammals except horses, the sprint is mainly the product of the lumbar spine. It can flex and extend by more than 50 degrees in the sprint, thus contributing more than 50 percent to stride length. (*Dogs in Motion* - Martin Fischer and Karin Lilje).

Clearly the spine needs to be a strong structure. It supports the ribs and internal organs that are suspended from it and the pelvis and pelvic limbs that are attached to it.

The Croup

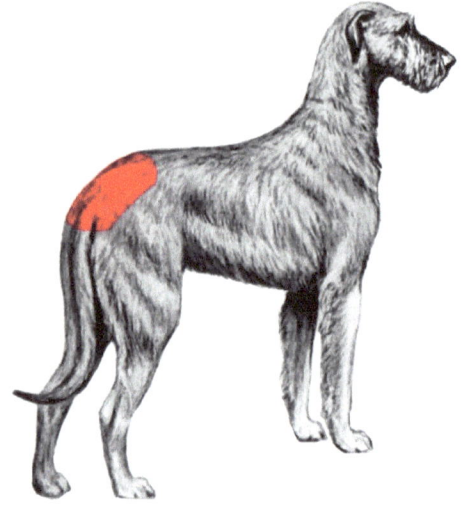

The area from the loin to the base of the tail is the dog's rump, referred to as the croup.

The croup pulls the feet and pelvic limbs under the body (pictured above), boosts the center of gravity for fast turns during the initial part of the stride, then sends the power and thrust forward by extending the hind leg in the latter half. The relationship of steepness (inclined angle) of the croup to agility means speed and the ability to change direction quickly. A fairly long croup is generally associated with a good length of the hip.

The croup in the picture above is rotated downward placing the pelvic limbs under the body and therefore under the center of gravity. It provides power and thrust when the legs are extended.

The Sacrum

The sacrum is a single bone that has formed from three fused vertebrae at the top of the pelvis. It's part of the dog's *croup* and is located between the hip bones, or more specifically the crests of the ilium. It joins the pelvic limbs to the lumbar spine. Power or propulsion generated by the hind legs is transferred through the spine to the torso through the sacroiliac joint, which also plays a significant role as a shock absorber.

An Aussie scrambling the side of an embankment.

The Australian Shepherd's sloping croup empowers it to work sheep in mountain terrain and also enables the breed's ability for quick turning.

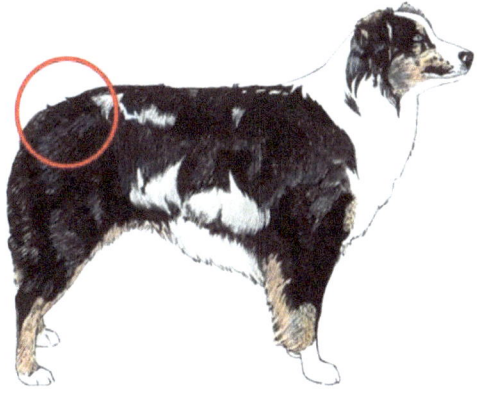

A dog with a sprinting-type drivetrain with a sloping croup is joined to a little steeper, longer pelvis. The longer pelvis and croup allow more area for the type of muscling necessary for quickness. The upper and lower thigh are wide and more heavily muscled. The sprinting drivetrain delivers speed to turn back runaways and also provides the specific action of the hock and stifle needed to low-heel cows and avoid kicks.

The croup of the dog built for sustained trotting is flatter than the sprinter. A flat croup, however, may indicate weaker loin muscles. In the conformation ring handlers often sculpt hair over the steeper croup of certain dogs to give the illusion of a flatter croup.

In review: The action in the hindquarters may be influenced significantly according to the angulation at which the sacrum is set on the pelvis in relation to the ground upon which the dog stands. The tail set will appear slightly lower than the topline when the sacrum is slightly angled.

The Tail

Tails provide counterbalance during locomotion and they reflect a general state of mind in dogs.

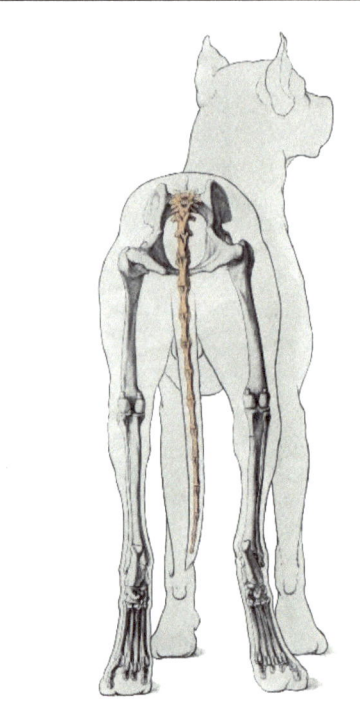

A caudal view of the caudal or coccygeal vertebrae.

The length of a dog's tail, the caudal vertebrae, can vary from a short natural bobtail with one or two vertebrae to a full-length tail with 23 vertebrae.

The angle of the pelvis and sacrum determines the tail set, which is governed by the muscle groups across the rump to the base of the tail.

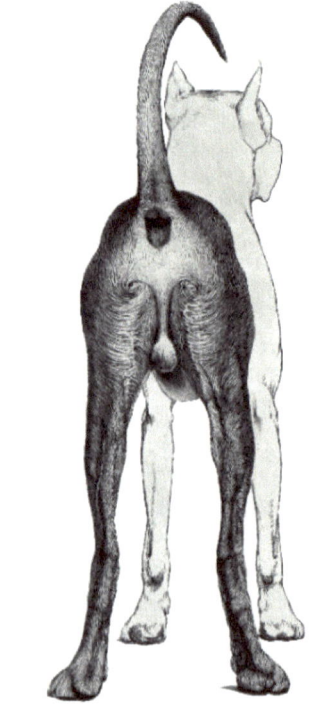

A caudal view of tail when elevated.

The dog with a shorter croup usually has a higher overall tail set, such as the Basset Hound pictured above. A low tail set indicates a longer croup. So, when a dog with a steeper pelvis carries its tail high it's going to be lower than a dog with a flat pelvis holding its tail high.

Note: There's a difference between *tail set* and *tail carriage*. The Border Collie pictured above illustrates a low tail set and carriage. The English Shepherd pictured below illustrates a short croup with higher tail carriage that expresses carefree behavior.

5 Forequarters

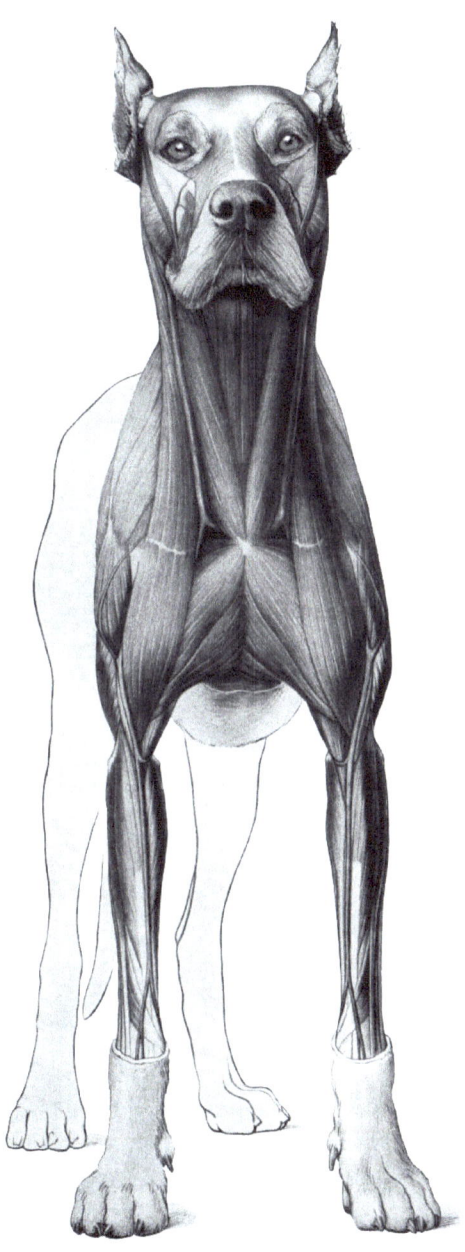

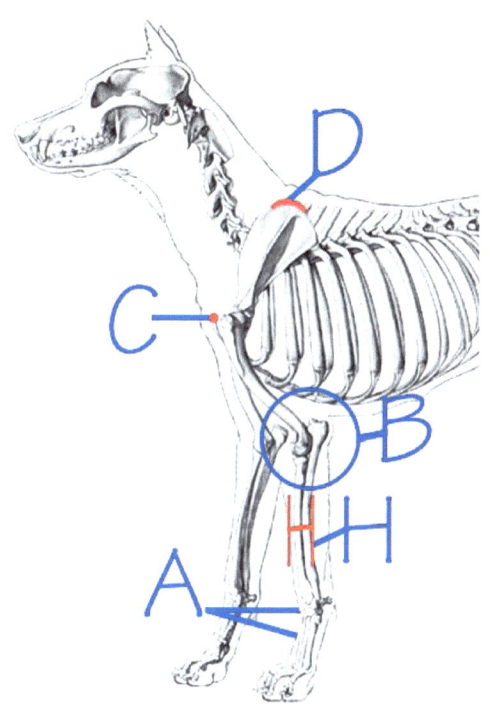

Forequarters or Thoracic Limbs

A: Pastern (carpals and metacarpals)
H: Radius and ulna (forearm)
B: Elbow joint
C: Point of shoulder
D: Point of withers (crest of scapular spine)

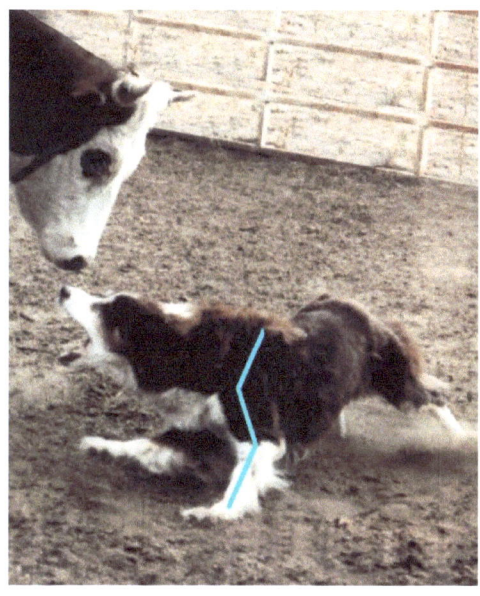

The front assembly is the mechanism for flexible steering and braking. It serves to stabilize and oppose lateral displacement, make turns, and control and lift the center of gravity. It can also play a role in propulsion like a vehicle in four-wheel drive.

Static Balance

For static, standing balance, the legs need to drop with a column of support beneath the pivot point of the front assembly. It's located in the upper mid scapula where it is attached to the body, which is also the weight bearing point for the front assembly.

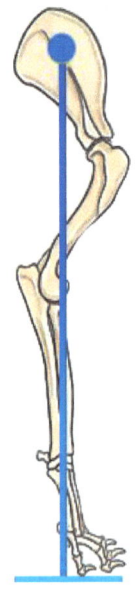

Let me reaffirm the point by saying, you should be able to drop a plumb line from the reciprocating center (upper midpoint) of the dog's shoulder through the vertical line of support to the metacarpal (palmar) pad. The slight angle of the pastern distributes the dog's weight on the metacarpal pad.

Center of Gravity

When the dog is standing naturally, it carries approximately 60% of its weight in the thoracic limbs. The back limbs carry approximately 40% of the weight. Therefore, the dog's static center of gravity is about mid-chest level behind the dog's shoulder blades.

The center of gravity (CG) is not a fixed point. It fluctuates according to the ratio of weight distribution between the front and hind end of the body. For example, the center of gravity is farther behind for breeds with longer backs like some terriers and corgis. However, the center of gravity in the Bulldog, with most of the weight of the body located in front of the midline, is more forward than the Sighthound breeds with well-developed loins and hindquarters. In the latter case, the center of gravity is consequently farther back.

The role played by the head and neck in maneuverability is highly significant in regulating and shifting the center of gravity. By moving the head and neck forward, the dog shifts its center of gravity forward. When negotiating turns, its head and neck lift up to draw the center of gravity back as opposed to propelling it forward. The kinetic center of gravity also moves forward when the dog carries an object with weight, such as a duck or dumbell.

There is significant strain on the forequarters when the head and neck are lowered to the ground, as with the Basset Hound scenting below.

When the dog travels uphill the center of gravity shifts toward the rear legs. Consequently, the forces are shifted to the front legs when the dog travels downhill. However, running down a steep grade, such as an Agility A-frame, may require dogs to shift their CG back towards the hind legs to keep from toppling over.

The hindquarters deliver propulsion and the forequarters provide support. They absorb the impact when the action (trotting, running, or jumping) is completed.

No Foot, No Dog

What about feet? The feet support the dog's entire body weight, with more than half of the dog's weight supported by the front feet. As a result, the front feet are slightly larger (broader) than the hind feet. Therefore, correct, sound feet are essential. Poor feet can limit athletic ability and lead to impaired performance and injury. A dog without sound feet is **not** sound and its usefulness is limited.

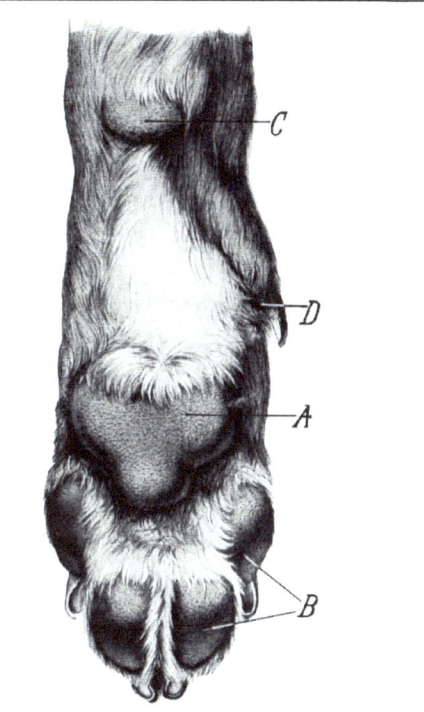

Parts of the thoracic foot:

A: Metacarpal or palmar pad (forelimbs) or metatarsal or plantar pad (hindlimbs)
B: Digital pads. The digits are numbered from one to five (1-5) from medial to lateral. For example, digit 1 (D) is the first digit, the dog's dewclaw.
C: Carpal pad.
D: Digital pad of first toe or the dewclaw (D-1)

Years ago, while on a judging assignment in Alaska, my dad and I had the opportunity to ride behind 20 Alaskan Huskies pulling a training gig, which was a Volkswagen Beetle chassis. My dad was sitting up front in the rig with Rick Outwin, who bred and trained dogs for the Iditarod, at the wheel. I stood on the back of the chassis hanging on as the dogs snaked through the forest. They were fast, very fast.

The dogs were moderate in structure, unlike much of what is seen in the conformation ring. I was impressed with the soundness of their feet.

While on that judging assignment, a nice Aussie puppy came in the ring, but hadn't been trained to walk on leash. After the show, I was asked by the ring steward if I knew who the woman was handling that entry? I told her, "I didn't." I was informed she was Natalie Norris of the world-class Anadyr Siberian sled dogs. When asked if I would like to meet her, of course, I jumped at the chance.

Norris, ever gracious, told me when their Siberian bitches had a litter, the Australian Shepherds would herd wandering puppies back to the safety of their mothers.

Norris' son, JP Norris, made observations that apply to dogs everywhere, even good stockdogs, not just those adapted to the conditions of the north.

"My ideal [feet pictured above right] is a dog that has been on the race team for the past four years and never had occasion to require any attention to his feet. No foot salve, no boots, just a lot of running through every kind of snow and water condition at extreme temperatures.

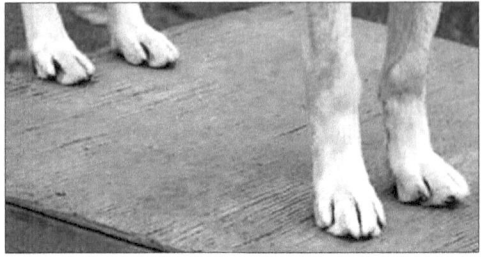

At the same time, some of the other Siberians in the kennel have required an occasional boot to heal a web crack or cut pad, not this boy," said JP.

Norris continued, "I think that the hair is of great importance. It must be thick and it must be coarse. Snow doesn't like to stick to this kind of hair. A foot like this is not a blanket immunity. Attention still has to be paid because there are conditions where snow will stick to anything."

Each foot has four digital pads and a large heart-shaped metacarpal or metatarsal pad. A carpal pad on the palmar region of the carpus and a functioning dewclaw with its associated pad to support the foot.

Some breed standards state: "Feet are oval shaped." The oval shaped foot is a semi-hare also known as a modified hare-foot. The oval shaped, **modified hare-foot** is the most functional type of foot for the breeds that need to be able to trot for certain distances, zig zag to change directions, stop abruptly or alter gait instantly in rugged terrain. The longer first and second phalanges of the third and fourth digital bones are also helpful for the type of quick initial speed needed for outrunning game during a hunt, heading off errant livestock, and negotiating turns in agility.

Traction is necessary for agility enabling quick turns and effective sprinting. Remember, in this instance, agility refers to nimbleness as opposed to the sport of agility. When the dog's foot makes ground contact, the most lateral part hits the surface first and then rotates inward. The dog's pads aid in traction. They cushion the initial impact, then the forces of the impact spread outward. The 3rd and 5th digital pads along with the metacarpal pad play a significant role in distributing forces during weight bearing and in storing or absorbing mechanical forces in the forequarters. The same principle applies for the rear digital and plantar pads. The metatarsal pad bearing a greater amount of weight than the front feet. Thickness is important for shock absorption and increased endurance. Resilience aids in flexibility. Uneven wear on the dog's pads themselves will reveal unbalances in gait. If the palmar pad is not sharing the weight with the digital pads, then they are carrying an extra burden. This will strain the toes causing early breakdown.

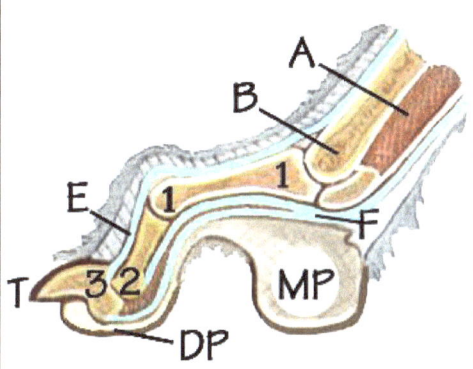

Lateral or side view of the cross-section of a digit or toe:

A: Muscle
B: Metacarpal (forelimb) or Metatarsal bone (hindlimb)
1: Proximal (1st) Phalanx of the digit which connects to the metacarpus/metatarsus
2: Middle (2nd) Phalanx of the digit
3: Distal (3rd) Phalanx which is covered by the claw or toenail. Between the toenail and bone of the distal phalanx there is a very vascular connective tissue, the dermis (corium)
MP: Metacarpal or palmar pad (forelimbs) or metatarsal or plantar pad (hindlimbs)
DP: Digital Pad
T: Claw or toenail
E: Extensor tendon that runs on top of the toes (highlighted in cyan)
F: Flexor tendon that runs beneath the toes (highlighted in cyan)

"The paw is made up of four digits and the metapodial [the distal portion of the dog's forelimb] region. This allows for the impact forces to spread out and be absorbed by individual components. The most lateral digit pad hits first and the third digit bears the greatest amount of impact force followed closely by the metacarpal pad. In the rear paws the fifth and third digit bear the greatest amount of the impact forces with the metatarsal pad bearing a higher amount than the front paws." – Robert Gillette, DVM, MSE, DACVSMR, *Athletic & Working Dog: Functional Anatomy and Biomechanics*

Strong ligaments and tendons usually hold the digits firmly in their positions. The toes are moved by digital extensor and flexor tendons. The tendons are strong but flexible and elastic connective tissues. Sometimes, the foot ligaments and tendons weaken. Weak feet (splayed, flat, and broken down) caused by weak connective tissue are more easily affected by rough, uneven terrain. Splayed and flat feet are serious problems because they cause early breakdown and lameness. Splayed feet expose the webbing to injury. What causes feet to splay? The tendons and ligaments that hold the digits together are lax, so the toes spread apart. It's generally an inherited defect but can be caused by an injury. When that happens, it will appear in the injured foot only, not the other feet. Long toenails can increase force placed on the toes (digits) and predispose them to fractures and other injuries.

The shorter third digital bones resulting in the cat-like foot (a deep, round foot with toes nearer the base of the heel of the foot) are a benefit to the trotting specialist. It requires less energy to operate (less power to lift); but it lacks adequate leverage necessary for unusual agility (ability to change direction or alter gait instantly), which is a hallmark for performance dogs. The modified hare-foot appears to be somewhat flatter than the compact, highly arched, cat-like foot. However, too often judges confuse the slightly flatter toes of the elongated hare foot with flat and broken-down feet. Flat, broken-down feet lack sufficient padding and spring. Splayed feet should also be penalized harshly.

Foot pads on the ground surface should be thick and resilient. Why? The foot pads are where the "rubber meets the road." This padding—fibrous, fatty cushions—are covered on the ground surface by a very hard toughened form of skin that is important for traction, shock absorption to reduce ground impact, and for protection from rocky surfaces, briars, thorns, frozen ground, and ice granules, etc. Thick pads also protect their feet from frostbite.

Separating Fact from Fiction

Are webbed feet a trait unique to certain breeds?

Actually, all dogs have webbing between their toes. The well-developed webbed feet in breeds like the

Otterhound increase propelling power when swimming and working on marshy terrain.

In review, the dog's feet deliver:

- Base of support
- Cushion to absorb shock
- Traction for starting
- Brakes for stopping
- Ability to paddle for swimming

Wrist and Front Pasterns

The metacarpal bones of the pastern need to be short, thick, but strong and flexible enough to reduce concussion when running, jumping, and turning.

The bones of the wrist, or carpus, the seven small round carpals (wrist joint), that connect the radius and ulna to the long part of the pastern, the metacarpals. They work in conjunction with the feet to provide lift to the front assembly to absorb external forces (shock) when the foot meets the ground. This in turn minimizes the stress to the bones that form the toes. When the dog is standing—facing the viewer—the forelegs are straight and perpendicular to the ground. It's perfectly normal for a dog to stand with the toes turned *slightly* to the sides for stability. It is **not** the same as a rotational or angular limb deformity in the carpus (wrist) or metacarpus causing an outward alignment of the toes or "toeing out," which is a fault.

The pasterns (pictured below) must be strong with the right amount of spring and give. Long, weak or broken-down pasterns do not give adequate support to the rest of the leg. Pasterns that are too lax (too much slope) or weak will lead to fatigue and predispose the dog to hyperextension and injury of the pasterns and knees at fast speeds. Ultimately, they will break down, especially as dogs age.

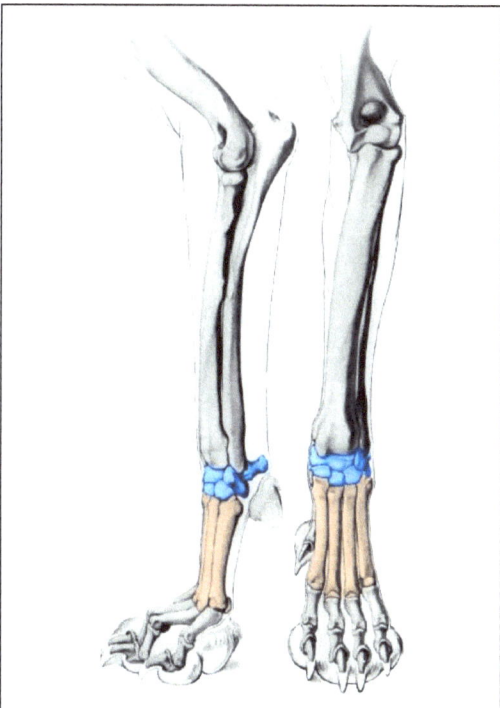

Lateral and cranial views of the carpus (blue) and the metacarpals (beige).

When viewed from the side there should be a slight angle. I like the definition of *slightly* found in the *Encyclopedia of K-9 Terminology*, "You are standing at the very edge of the Grand Canyon and you are told to move slightly forward." - Gilbert and Gilbert

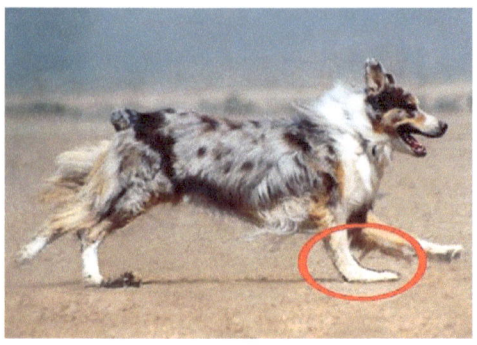

The carpal pad located on the inner surface of the front pastern area is important to the functionality of dogs in action. It stabilizes and reduces torque as it touches the ground to maintain balance (pictured above). It also cushions feet and thoracic limbs as the dog sprints and makes tight turns.

The carpal pad is associated with the dew claw. Dewclaws stabilize and help the dog maintain balance as the dog sprints and makes tight turns. Dewclaws on the front legs are attached to functioning tendons. The tendons are attached to muscles. Current research indicates that dogs without dewclaws have more foot injuries and are more prone to arthritis.

According to Juanita Ely, a rancher and the earliest documented Australian Shepherd breeder, "Some people cut off their [dog's] dew claws and they are the brakes for a dog going downhill. He has nothing to dig into the vegetation or ground covering to keep him from going head over heels and can get badly bruised and hurt. They also keep him from going too deep in crusted snow. 'I always think who would want to start downhill in a car without brakes; so why take the brakes off your dog?' Nature put them on for a reason and that's it!"

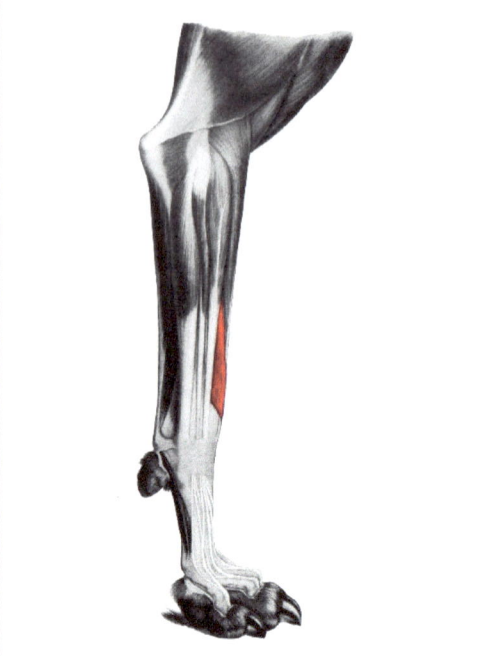

The abductor pollicis longus muscle is one of the extrinsic muscles of the front leg. It abducts the dewclaw. *Pollex* is Latin for thumb. Abductor pollicis longus translates to long abductor of the thumb.

The Forearm

The forearm is made up of the radius and ulna. They are fused together and operate as a single bone, but permit the dog to rotate the limb on its axis because they can roll past one another. The ulna is attached firmly at the elbow and loosely at the carpus (seven bones of the wrist). The radius has the opposite arrangement. Muscles and ligaments between the two bones keep the limb intact. The tibia and fibula in the hind assembly operate in the same way.

The elbow is the lower articular surface of the humerus and the upper extension of the radius and ulna (forearm). It's attached to the thorax by the pectoral muscles on both sides of the body. It's a hinge like structure that allows the elbow to flex (bend) by means of the biceps muscle. The origin of the biceps is at the front of the shoulder below the shoulder joint. It travels down the limb parallel with the humerus and inserts into the upper ends of the front of the radius and ulna. It also flexes the elbow and assists significantly in drawing the front leg forward. While the triceps muscle, which lies behind the shoulder, helps flex the shoulder and extends the elbow joint. The elbow joint is stabilized through mechanical constraints of the deep fascia and other soft tissues.

the plumb line drops from the shoulder through the middle of the carpus and continues on through the middle of the dog's paw.

<u>A dog is less apt to break down if its legs are in normal alignment</u>. Wear is evenly distributed in normal joints. But atypical wear is disproportionate. Rotational forces and compression on the surface of the joints leads to unnecessary wear and tear culminating in osteoarthritis. It ultimately affects the dog's soundness and state of well-being.

Thoracic Limb Anomalies

When the dog's toes point inward toward the midline, it's a fault known as pigeon-toed. When they turn outwards, away from the midline, it's known as "east-west". These are the result of weak muscles, ligamentous

Normal Articulation

Correct foot placement reflects normal limb development. On normal limbs, joint laxity, humeral articulation and/or a rotational abnormality. When rotation of the limbs, also known as torsion, is not involved, the irregularity is called an angular limb deformity (ALD).

Limb deformities are not unusual in dogs, but the cause is not always easy to pinpoint. They are often multifaceted including the origin and degree of deviation. What may look like an irregularity in the carpus or elbow can be a combination of angular and rotational components. ALDs are generally classified as either varus (toward the midline) or valgus (outward deviation). The terminology is Latin for twisted or bent and crooked.

> **Note**: It is normal for an immature dog to stand with its toes slightly out. As the dog matures and the ribs spring, the limbs will typically straighten out.

The dog's growth plates (physes) are the soft, spongy, non-calcified cells near the ends or tops of the long bones, where new bone forms. They are the weakest part of the bone and are easily damaged with rigorous exercise during developmental stages. Incomplete ossification and fractures to the growth plates can result in limb deformities and osteoarthritis. The upper front leg (the humerus) and the thigh bone (the femur) are particularly susceptible to injury. The growth plates close at approximately month 10 in smaller breeds and month 14 in larger breeds.

Unequal growth of the bones of the foreleg (the radius and ulna) can occur when the growth plates of the lower forelimb are disrupted—causing one of the bones to stop growing prematurely, which forces the paired bone, usually the ulna that is still growing, to bend and twist. It can result from physical injury or as a result of genetics. It's most obvious in dogs with chondrodysplasia, otherwise known as canine dwarfism, which is characteristic of certain breeds, such as the Corgi and Dachshund.

The Shoulder

The shoulder is often referred to as the cornerstone of the front assembly. The shoulder joint where the humeral head articulates with the much smaller socket of the scapula is attached to the skeleton by a sling of soft tissue (muscle, tendons, and fibrous sheets of fascia) unlike the ball-and-sockets of the pelvis, which are linked to the spine by the sacrum. The muscles and ligaments unite the scapulae to the spine as well as to the ribs and allows freedom of movement.

The scapulae are the center of rotation for the thoracic limbs. They work like a pendulum. The actual shoulder joint moves very little while the dog is in motion. The musculature of the shoulder is capable of flexion, extension, rotation, abduction and adduction and is mobile in all directions, which enables greater stride length for running and jumping.

Shoulder Layback

The front-to-back sloping of the shoulder blade is referred to as ***layback***. This terminology is rooted in the equine world where well-laid-back shoulders are desirable for a smooth riding horse.

While there are many comparisons that can be made between the anatomy of horses and dogs, there is one significant difference. <u>Dogs have flexible backs, as compared to the horse's relatively rigid and inflexible back,</u> and, most importantly, dogs are not ridden. This is due to the shape of the interconnecting surfaces of the thoracic vertebrae that limit upward and downward movement of the horse's spine.

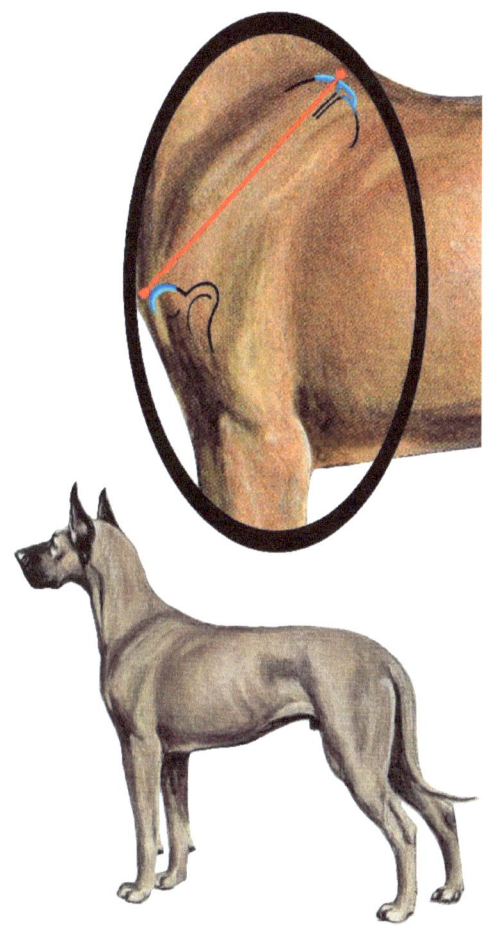

Many dog show judges use palpable points on the outer surface to evaluate shoulder angulation as the dog stands. It's done by touching the point of shoulder—which is actually the tip of the humerus, not the end of the scapula—with the finger of one hand. Then touching the highest point of withers with the index finger of the other hand. Anatomically speaking, the withers may be a tiny bit higher than the rest of the back because of the nature of the thoracic vertebrae. This will reveal an approximate angle that will be about three to five degrees greater than the true angle.

Shoulder angulation is not static and it can change based on muscle tone and the quality of connective tissue and stance.

Shoulder Lay-in

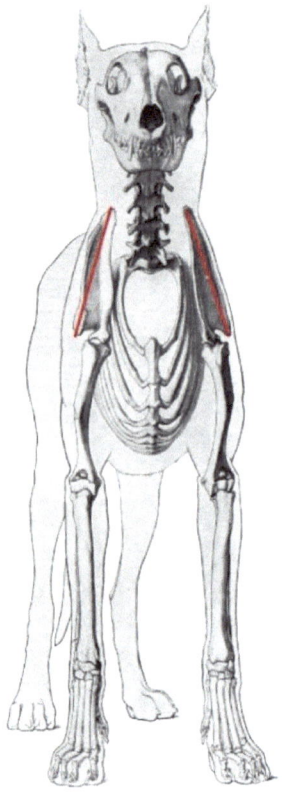

Shoulder **lay-in** means the shoulder blades tilt toward each other. The width of the withers (upper scapular edges) should be sufficiently narrow for adequate inclination of the blades over well-sprung ribs, while allowing ample room for muscling between the withers.

If there is too little distance between the upper tips of the scapulae, they may interfere with each other causing the dog discomfort and perhaps hindering the dog's ability to lower its head to eat or pick up an object without splaying its legs laterally. You can place your hands on the dog to feel the width between the scapular tips.

Separating Fact from Fiction

Is the well laid back 45-degree shoulder angle described in a number of breed standards the ideal layback for maximum reach and drive?

The 45-degree angle of the static shoulder is imaginary. It's a myth. It has been proven through cineradiography (moving X-rays). So, even if it does exist as a description in a breed standard, it is a misnomer. It is **nonexistent** in real, living dogs. The shoulder is not set in concrete. It's dynamic and moves forward and backward by an array of muscles and is not limited by a stationary position. The highly flexible spine and its muscles also come into play when the dog is in motion.

In her book, *Dogsteps: A New Look,* Rachel Page Elliott addressed why a 45-degree angle of the shoulder blade is only a myth in contradiction to the many writings that describe such an angle is essential to ideal conformation. She wrote, "There is a human tendency to accept what appears in print as having withstood some incredible truth test. A case in point is the long-held belief that a 45-degree slope of the shoulder blade is necessary for providing maximum extension or reach of the forelimb, and this is written into many breed standards. I have often wondered about the elusiveness of this detail, for I have never found it myself, and it was not until given the opportunity to observe skeletal action through moving x-rays or cineradiography that I realized why such a position would be a mechanical impossibility to the dog's function. A 45-degree slant, or layback, would be workable if the blade were a stationary bone with a more or less fixed joint from which the upper arm moved forward and back. Actually, this is not the case."

Elliott continues, "What we have failed to recognize is the great mobility of the shoulder blade as a partner of the upper arm, which serves as a lever in lifting and transporting the central body forward as smoothly as possible."

Separating Fact from Fiction

A popular belief exists that is often applied in the dog show world that straighter shoulder layback is synonymous with pounding and faulty movement because it restricts reach. But it's a misconception!

The angulations of working and performance dogs are more conservative than the well-laid-back shoulder blade on their conformation cousins. Dogs built for quick, light and easy movement have slightly steeper shoulders (reduced angles at the shoulder and elbow and at the knee and hock), with also less slope to the pasterns.

Consider the Belgian Malinois. They are recognized for their rapid acceleration and ability to turn quickly. They lean toward straighter front and rear assemblies. This gives them tremendous agility. <u>To be absolutely clear</u>, we are **not** talking about straight angulations like the Chinese Shar-Pei or Chow Chow breeds that are not built to execute a 180-degree rollback at a sprint or jump.

Faulty movement occurs when the forequarters are **not** in balance with hindquarters. When the front and rear assembly are in sync and balanced unto itself, the gait will be coordinated regardless of the angulation of its skeletal members.

The front assembly needs to be coordinated with the hind assembly. In other words, the angulation of the forequarters <u>**must**</u> correspond with the angulation of the hindquarters. Correctness has to be defined by function. If we look at the stockdog's job description we discover they depend on quick bursts of speed to sprint ahead, stop abruptly with a simultaneous rollback to turn back livestock and then drop down low enough to avoid being kicked.

Dogs bred for sustained, endurance trotting have more shoulder layback and a little more slope to the front pastern than their sprinting counterparts. But that has been taken to an extreme, also. Breeds such as the Siberian Husky that are used in the grueling 1,100-mile Iditarod race are much more moderate than their counterparts in the conformation ring. Generally speaking, show dogs are not bred from a utility perspective, but purely to win dogs shows. They also could not function with the unsupported feet and tipped-up toes (see page 79) as often seen winning in the conformation ring.

Separating Fact from Fiction

In the dog show world the apparent length of the upper arm is measured from the point of shoulder to the point of the elbow (olecranon process). Another popular belief exists that short upper arms shorten stride.

Furthermore, Edward Gilbert along with Thelma Brown state in *K-9 Structure and Terminology*, "Long upper arms increase reach."

Dr. Peter Friedrich, President of the German Kennel Club wrote, "One of the most widely propagated explanations for short-strided, ineffective restricted seeming forelimb movement in the trot is the assumption that the upper arm is disproportionately short."

How does that measure in the real world? Scientists at the University of Jena using high definition cameras provide insight into the locomotion of dogs, especially regarding the proportions of the forelimbs of the dog breeds examined using a uniform, comparable analysis of results.

When a terrier "goes to ground" it is not so different from a herding dog (below) dropping down to low heel a cow or to play.

They found the measurements confirm that the forelimbs of all breeds consist of two relatively uniform segments, the upper arm and the pastern, and two variable segments, the shoulder blade and the forearm.

Moreover, proportions of the front legs were nearly identical in all breeds— although "it is clear that the upper arm of a Schnauzer is shorter than that of a Great Dane," according to Professor Dr. Martin S. Fischer of the Jena study.

The total length of a foreleg is always exactly 27 percent. Whereas the relative length of the shoulder blade varies between 24 and 34 percent. "The shoulder blade of short legged dogs is relatively long and that of greyhounds is relatively short. <u>But the length of the upper arm always stays the same</u>."

Side note: The research at Jena University also revealed when the dog is in motion—the position of the scapula and the forearm parallel each other as if linked. "If the forearm is in a vertical position, then the shoulder blade will be in the same position."

Pectorals

The dog is highly flexible in nearly any direction. The thoracic or forelimbs are enabled to reach farther forward during the gallop by a stronger forward rotation of the shoulder.

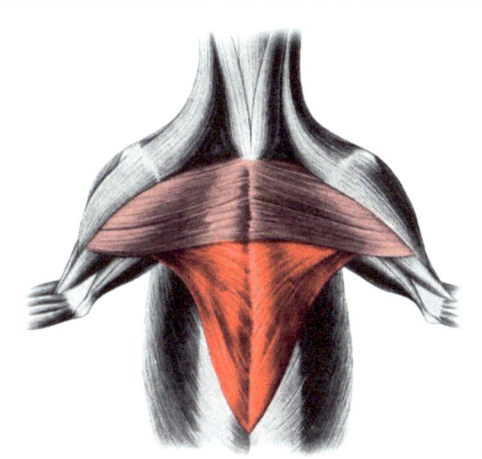

Above: Ventral view revealing the superficial pectoral muscle in bright red and the deep or ascending pectoral muscle in pink. **Below:** Lateral and cranial views of the dog showing the pectoral muscles.

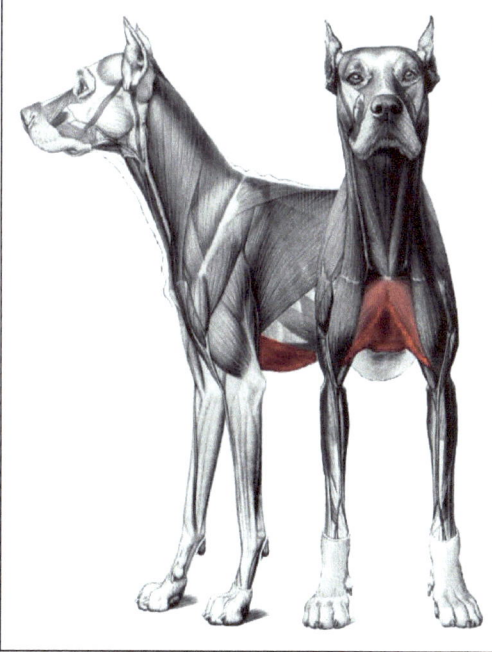

The pectoral muscles connect the front of the chest with the upper arm and shoulder and move the chest forward over the advanced limb and prevent the limb from being abducted during weight bearing.

They play a considerable part in forelimb movement, but not an active part in forward movement. They provide major aid in lateral shifts. They also extend the shoulder joint and draw the thoracic limb backwards during locomotion. The dog pictured above is making a lateral shift by abducting or moving the bones away from the body's midline.

Likewise, the above illustrates a dog using a lateral shift to change directions except it's using muscles for adducting or moving the bones toward the body's midline. The thoracic limbs crisscross each other.

On the Diagonal (Down and Back)

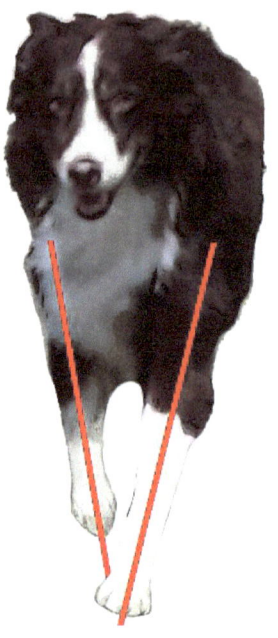

As the dog trots toward the viewer, the feet converge toward the mid-point or under the body (line of gravity). The thoracic limbs from the shoulder to paw, resemble a "V" shape as the dog's legs are drawn underneath in the trotting gait. The center of gravity passes through the radius and ulna to the pasterns to the feet. The heel or metacarpal pads must originate in a perpendicular line under the center of weight bearing.

Deviations from normal alignment, such as anomalies of the cuboidal bones of the carpus, are problematic because abnormal forces predispose dogs to orthopedic problems, such as osteoarthritis. All of which contribute to gaiting faults. Why? Because they negatively affect the joints and they alter the way the forces are loaded and distributed throughout limbs and feet.

Convergence occurs in the show ring or while herding sheep or at the end of a long day working cattle on a ranch.

In ranch country or when out jogging

with their owners, dogs can travel over hard surfaces, such as sunbaked earth that can send shockwaves through their joints. Dogs that are over-angulated are much more at risk for injury.

Grasslands, though soft on impact, can actually make the muscles work hard. The ground can be uneven, slippery or muddy when wet.

When dogs encounter rough, unstable terrain like rock-strewn gravel, they have to be able to recover quickly. Those stressors make their way up the dog's joints, which is why correct, sound feet and legs are so very important.

A dog that is able to converge while trotting transfers into the ability to turn off the centerline increasing quickness.

Notice the Australian Shepherd and the wolf; both are single tracking.

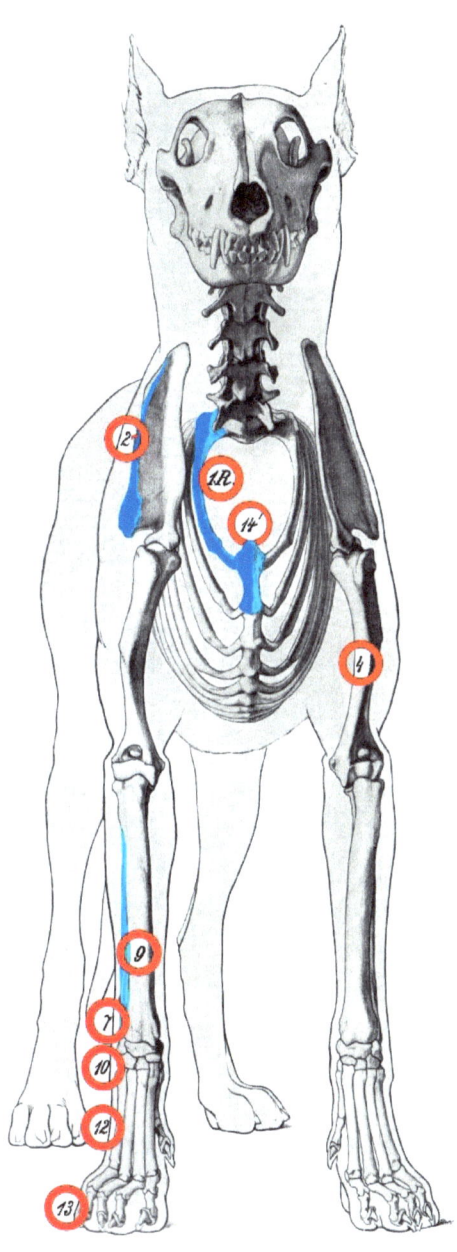
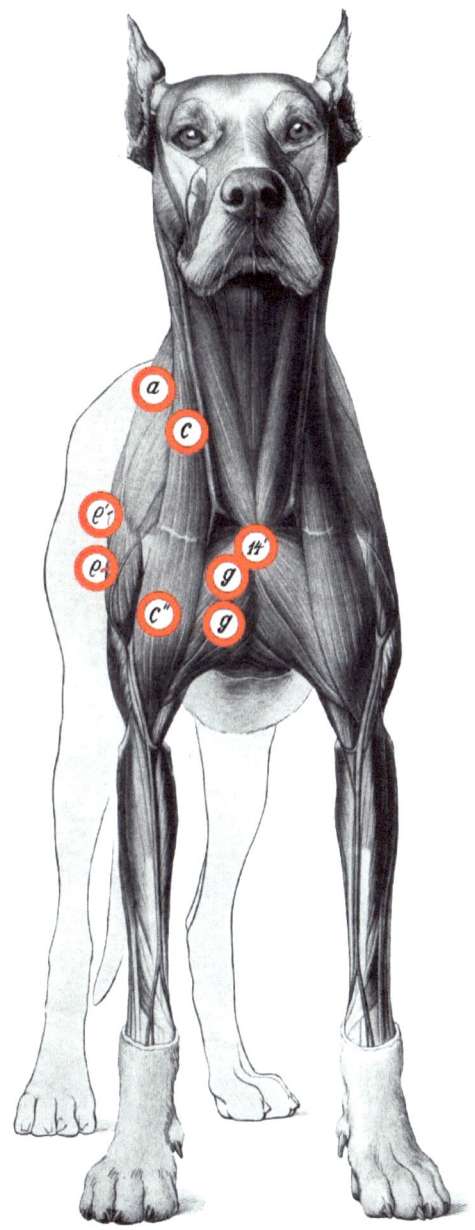

From the top to bottom:
2 – Scapular spine (marked in blue)
1R – First rib (marked in blue)
14' – Manubrium (marked in blue)
4 – Humerus
9 – Radius
7 – Ulna (highlighted in cyan).
10 – Carpus
12 – Metacarpus
13 – Phalanges

Left side: From the top to bottom:
a.- Trapezius
e, e' – Deltoids

Middle left:
c, c'' - Brachiocephalicus

Middle: from top to bottom:
14' – Manubrium
g, g' – Pectorals (superficial and deep)

For Fun

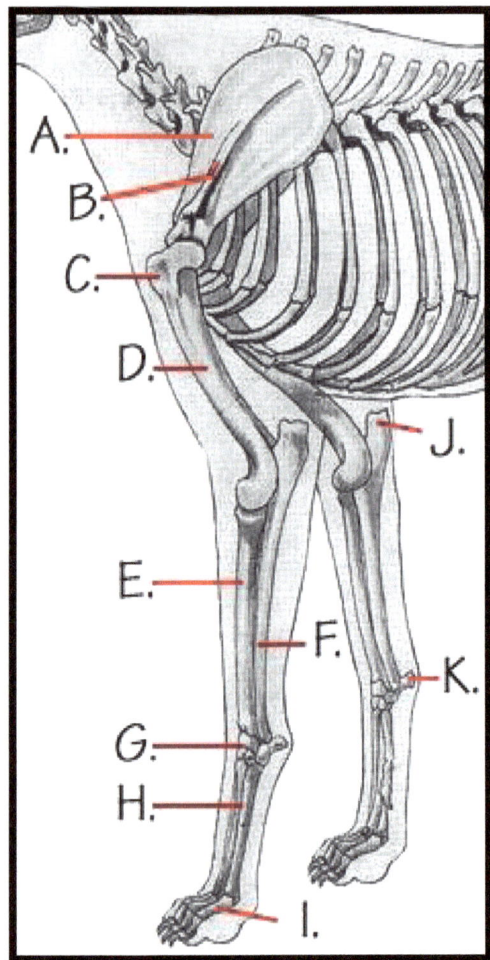

Match the anatomical parts to their corresponding letters:

Scapular spine	
Point of shoulder	
Ulna	
Scapula	
Wrist	
Radius	
Olecranon process	
Digits	
Humerus	
Pastern	
Carpal pad	

Can you name the underlying bones for the front assembly?

Shoulder
a.
Upper arm
b.
Forearm
c.
Front pastern
d.

Answers to Match the parts:

A. Scapula (Shoulder blade).
B. Scapular Spine.
C. Point of shoulder.
D. Humerus (Upper arm).
E. Radius.
F. Ulna.
G. Wrist (Carpus / Carpal bones).
H. Pastern (Metacarpals).
I. Digits (Foot).
J. Olecranon (Tip of ulna).
K. Carpal pad.

Answers to name the underlying bones:

a. – Scapula (Shoulder).
b. – Humerus (Upper arm).
c. – Radius and Ulna (Forearm).
d. – Metacarpals (Front pastern.

6 - The Hindquarters

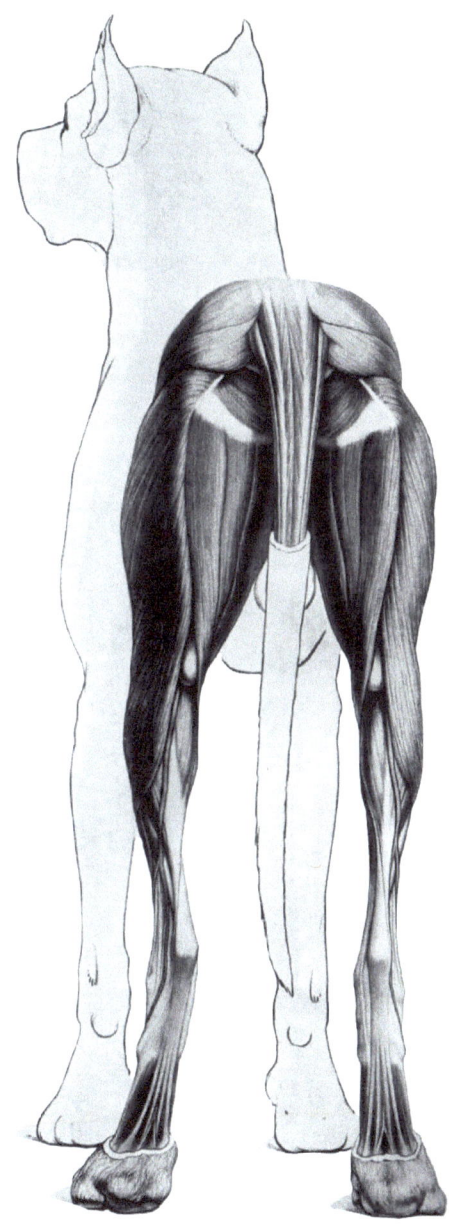

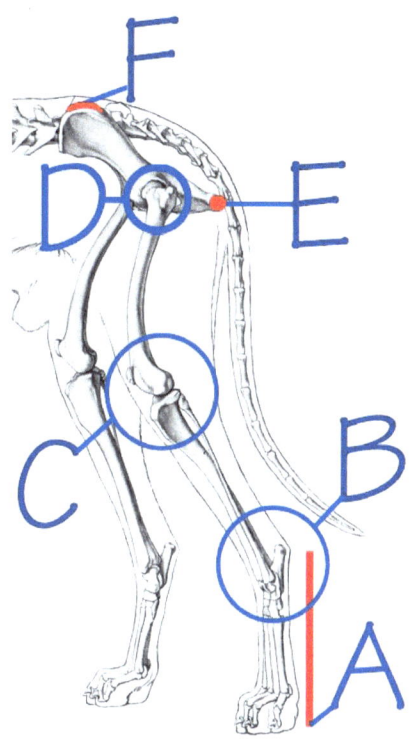

Hindquarters or Pelvic Limbs

A: Rear pastern (metatarsi) sometimes referred to as the hock
B: Hock (tarsal) joint
C: Stifle joint (knee)
D: Hip joint and the center of gravity
E: Point of buttock (ischial tuberosity)
F: Point of hip (iliac crest)
E to F: The hip

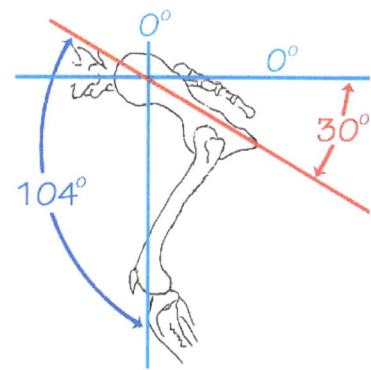

What happens in the neck starts in the back, and what happens in the back starts in the pelvic or hind limbs. The rear is the engine that provides energy and enables quick, sharp turns, and the ability to rollback and run in the opposite direction.

You can use different types of angle finders including a goniometer to take specific measurements of dogs and their thoracic and pelvic limb angulations, but it's tedious and impractical. Instead, it's far more important to focus on overall balance and soundness.

To see how well the dog is balanced, it's necessary for the rear pasterns to be **vertical** to the ground (above) with the weight evenly distributed at the four corners of its body instead of in a rocking horse stance, also known as *bracing*—when the dog's legs are positioned like an "A" frame (below).

As previously mentioned, the pelvis is attached to the vertebrae of the lumbar spine through the sacrum. The highly flexible lumbosacral joint is the articulation or junction between the last lumbar vertebrae and the sacrum. It is the most mobile joint in the vertebral column enabling flexion and extension movements with lateral and rotational movements to a lesser degree.

The lower limbs are linked to the pelvis at the hip joint. The articular head of the femur is round and fits into the acetabulum, or hip socket, like a hand in a glove.

The rear assembly, the hindquarters, are designed for propulsion. They provide the driving power that thrusts the dog into action. Stability is key for driving power.

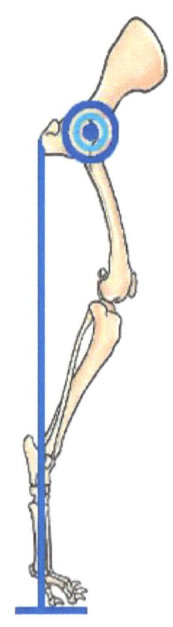

For static standing balance, the legs need to drop with the weight bearing point of the rear assemblies beneath the column of support. The metatarsus and pads of the foot under the point of the buttock (ischial tuberosity) provide linear stability, sudden stops, turn around efficiency or changes in direction, jumping and landing.

R. H. Smythe M.R.C.V.S. made clear why some dogs are able to function satisfactorily and why others do not. "In the original hind limbs, the line of force impinging upon the circular acetabulum was directed on to what may be termed a 10:30 position. In the angulated limb it is changed to nine o'clock and the femur which normally rotates in the acetabulum in clockwise position; now tends to proceed counterclockwise."

Dr. Smythe went on to say, "Of late years the tendency has been to demand angulation. This implies a flexed hip and stifle, extra length of the tibia and the shortening of the hindlimb from hock to foot."

He added, "During rest, the hind foot is then placed on the ground several inches behind a line dropped perpendicularly from the seat bone of the pelvis [point of buttock / ischial tuberosity] to the ground."

of propulsion possible and the change of shape has thrown an undue stress upon parts of the body never designed for the purpose."

He quantified "…lengthening the tibia in the Alsatian changed the direction in the application of power [and] has introduced some side-effects, not all to the good. In the first place, the thrust into the hip joint from the head of the femur has changed direction so that the line of force now encounters the rounded cup of the acetabulum [hip socket] at nearer nine o'clock where before it was nearer ten-thirty o'clock."

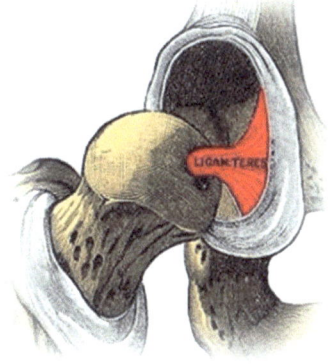

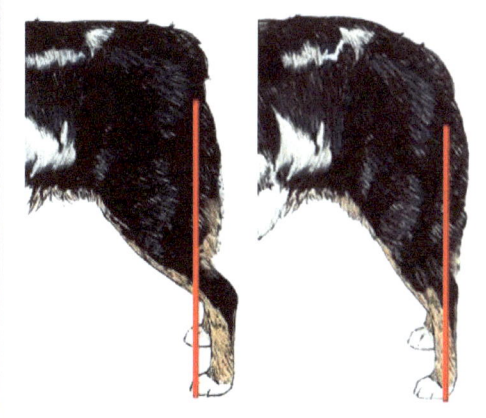

The trend for dog show judges to reward dogs with excessive angulation in conformation show rings began in the 1960s.

Smythe said, "This puts an additional strain on the short 'round ligament' [teres ligament], which holds the head of femur firmly in the acetabulum.

"It also necessitates a different pattern in the type of muscular activity which controls the hindlimb and directs its force onto the wall of the acetabulum. In the original type of dog, the pelvic muscles had the task of holding together the component parts of the hip joint, with comparatively short hind stride which produced very little movement of the head of the femur.

Smythe further emphasized, "The modern conformation dog has had to be reshaped in order to make this kind

"Today, in the angulated specimen, the hind foot moves forward from a considerable distance behind the body to an equally considerable distance in front of it. This throws a great deal more strain of the joint surfaces."

Moderate angulation is the normal, most practical for dogs for two reasons. Hindquarters with greater angulation are less stable because they lack vertical support, so there's a bigger risk for injury—hyperextension of joints including cruciate ligament injuries. The cruciate ligament attaches the tibia to the femur. If it ruptures, it causes lameness and instability. Is it coincidental in the sharp rise of cruciate surgeries in many popular breeds?

> "In running dogs such as the Greyhound, the change [more angulation], whatever it has produced in the matter of appearance, has certainly done nothing to improve performance. The racing Greyhound of today has a straight hindlimb and tibia of moderate length and it executes a large number of short, rapid strides, attaining a very high speed.
>
> The exhibition Greyhound with exaggerated angulation, "Standing over a lot of ground," and with a very much longer hind stride, both behind and beneath the body, actually carrying the hind feet past the shoulders in the forward section of the stride, cannot catch the smaller dog with the straighter, stifle and hock, simply because the fewer, longer strides cannot compete with the many shorter ones." - R. H. Smythe

To recap, the dog has more accuracy for foot placement when the plumb line drops from the point of buttocks to the ground. The metatarsus and foot are under the pelvis, and the dog is able to gather itself and turn more sharply than its counterpart with extended angulation. Because their hind feet are out behind the body there is less support for quick turns and traversing difficult terrain.

The Stifle

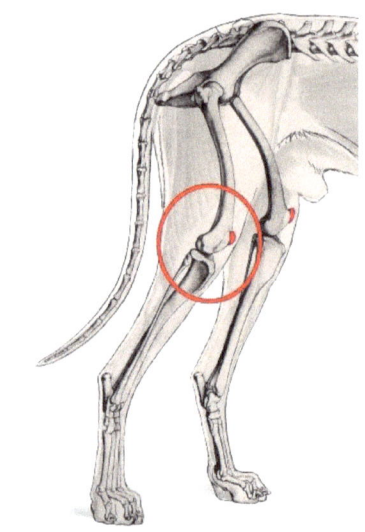

The stifle or knee joint (tibiofemoral joint) is the angle made between the upper thigh (femur) and the lower thigh. The patella (in red) is a sesamoid bone that is embedded within the tendon of the quadriceps muscle group. It becomes the patellar ligament attaching to the tibia.

The gastrocnemius muscle of the lower thigh controls the degree of flexion of the stifle and the tarsal joint. The tibia is comparable to the human shin bone. It lies directly under the skin, with no muscle covering.

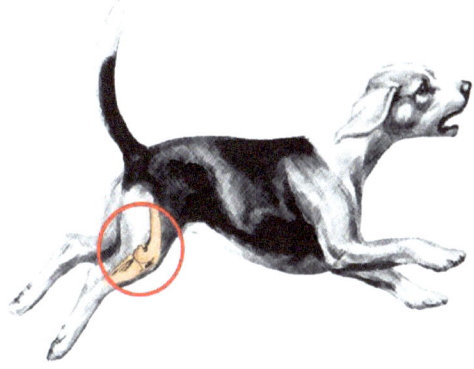

As the dog moves, the patella (like our knee cap) slides over the stifle joint. When the extensor apparatus is correctly aligned with the underlying skeleton, the patella is stable and acts as a pulley, directing the line of action for the quadriceps tendon.

In his book *Dog in Action*, McDowell Lyon wrote, "This is the influence behind every request for well-bent stifles, but runs into a natural heritage difficulty which causes the bones between the stifle and hock to shorten as this one lengthens. In both the front and back leg, we have this trouble, which was long ago recognized by horsemen."

Lyon goes on to explain how Lacog, a French authority of the last century, says of the horse's front leg, "The length of the forearm varies inversely with that of the cannon bone." In other words, as one got long the other became shorter, writes Lyon. He concluded by saying, 'This tends to show that nature has her own ideas about bone relation and tries to balance them out to that idea."

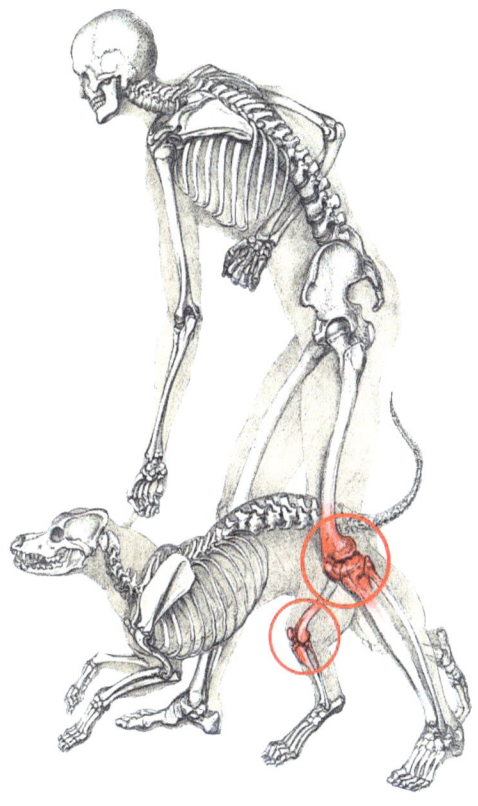

Point of interest. The dog's stifle is comparable to the human knee and to the horse's stifle, but there is one main difference and it's fascinating. Horses have a stay apparatus. This enables them to lock their limbs in place and allows them to sleep while standing up. It's located in the horse's stifle and forequarters. The stay apparatus works because when the stifle is locked in place the hock and fetlock reciprocate.

The horse's reciprocal mechanism is made up of the superficial flexor tendon, peroneus tertius and gastrocnemius, which causes the horse's stifle, hock, and fetlock to lock or flex or extend in unison. When the stifle bends, the hock and fetlock match the action.

Furthermore, according to G.H. Wentink in his 1976 paper, *Dynamics of the hind limb at walk in horse and dog*, states, "The tendinous interosseous and superficial digital flexor muscle of the horse store elastic energy at impact and use this energy to stretch the peroneus tertius tendon, the energy ultimately being used to flex the hock at lifting; the superficial digital flexor and the peroneus tertius tendons coordinate the movements of stifle and hock during the swing phases; all the components mentioned save energy: the horse is an animal built for great stamina; in the dog, the analogue of the aforementioned tendons are muscular; consequently the dog is able to dig its digits and claws into the ground for a strong grip and great friction; the digitigrade dog is adapted and for great speed."

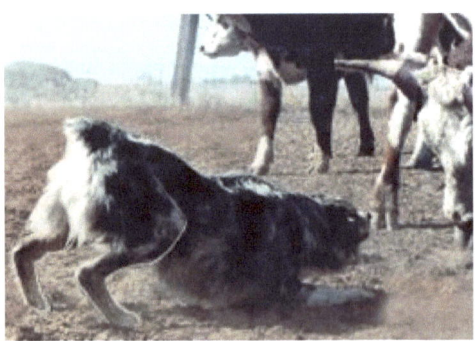

The previously mentioned study at Jena University confirmed when the dog is in motion, the angle of the dog's femur (thigh) is matched by the top of the metatarsus like a *pantograph*—a mechanical instrument that produces identical movements, such as for scale drawing (pictured to the right). The position of the femur is mirrored by the rear pastern at touchdown and lift off.

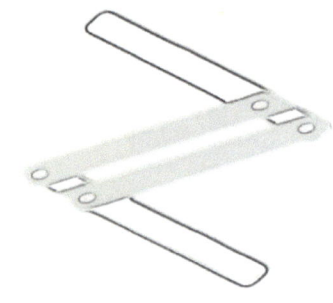

The pantographic action of the dog's femur is matched within five degrees variance by the movement in the top of rear pasterns (metatarsi).

The rear assembly requires much more muscular strength especially when twisting and turning in deep sand, heavy snow, thick mud, and on uneven terrain.

The rear assembly drives the dog into position transmitting power from the hindquarters through the loin to the forequarters. Notice the only point of contact pictured (above) is the dog's hind foot.

The law of physics comes into play because poor angles put more stress on joints and may lead to compensations throughout the entire limb including the feet.

The athletic Whippet, the smallest of the Sighthounds, owes its speed, grace, and type to its big brother, the Greyhound. Likewise, the Australian Shepherd, a medium-size stockdog, requires moderate angulation to avoid injuries when launching and landing, such as catching Frisbees high in the air. The same concept applies to the Golden Retriever used for hunting or any dog with an active lifestyle.

Willingness to please and "heart" are paramount in top performance dogs. These traits are embedded deep in the dog's neural mechanisms through selective breeding.

"My three-legged dog, Maty, was the first and only tripod to qualify and compete in a World's Canine Disc Championship. She competed in the Worlds twice to prove it wasn't a fluke!" – Lynne Ouchida

Force is generated when the hind foot strikes the ground then drives through the hock up the tibia and is transmitted to the pelvis at the socket of the hip joint (acetabulum), which is also the pivot point of the pelvic limbs, and then onward to the spine through the sacrum.

The Hock

The tarsus, or hock joint, like our ankle joint, is strong and multifaceted. It connects the tibia and fibula (calf bone) with the tarsal bones.

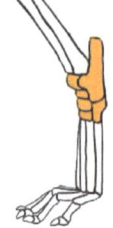

It's made up of seven tarsi, the group of small bones, that are arranged in two staggered rows. It's supported by tarsal ligaments that are extremely important to the normal function of the joint.

When viewed from the rear, the hocks should be parallel and perpendicular to each other.

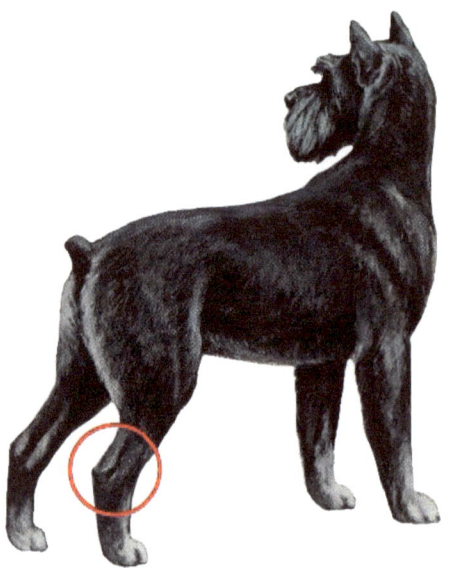

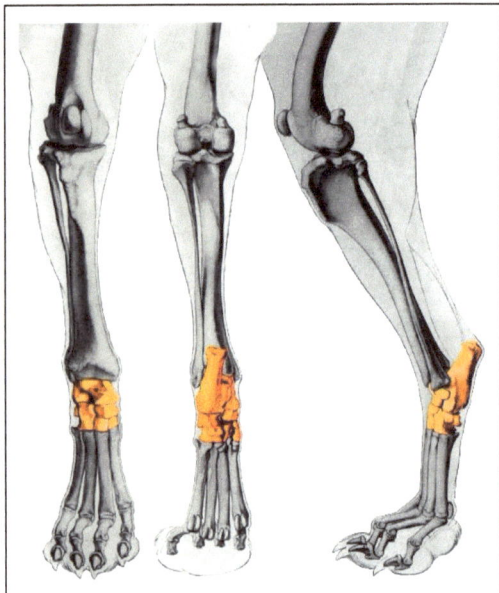

Cranial, caudal and lateral views of the tarsus (in orange).

When the hock, or tarsal joint, (pictured above) is correctly angled it places the rear foot under the vertical line of support in the rear assembly. This is optimal for stability and rapid turning.

The hocks have a good range of motion. They naturally flex and bend during propulsion. The articulation between the tibia and the talus (cannon bone) is the utmost important for thrust. But joints are only as strong as the ligaments that stabilize them. If the joint hyperextends (bends forward) or is easily pushed forward when the dog is standing, which is generally caused by laxity in the ligaments that hold them together, it creates instability.

thigh. It becomes the Achilles tendon that is attached to the point of hock to prevent or determine the degree of flexion, especially in jumping and sprinting.

The length of the metatarsi - from the hock joint to the ground - is determined by a ratio of hock height (ground to tarsal joint) to shoulder height. The average length of hock in performance dogs is 1:3 to 1:3.3. Well let-down or short metatarsi that are closer to the ground are **not** designed for the ability to change direction, swerve and feint or alter gait instantly. They lack the needed leverage.

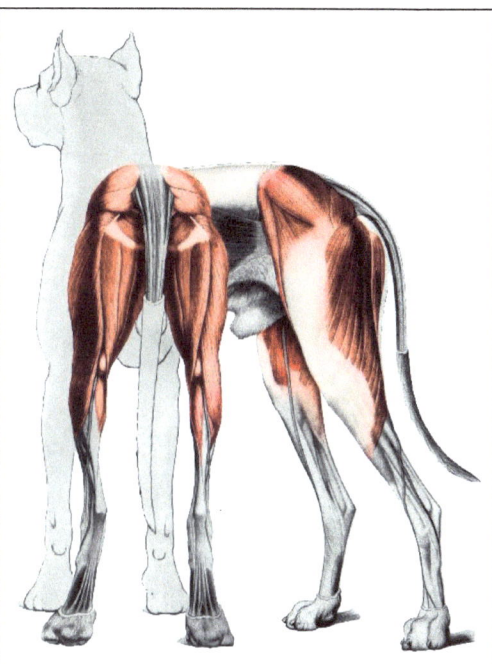

Lateral and caudal views of the rearing muscles above, and a dorsal view, pictured below.

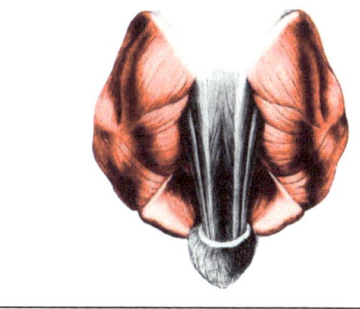

The gastrocnemius, or calf muscle, is a powerful antigravity muscle located at the hinder part of the lower or second

Well-developed rearing muscles are essential to produce the quick bursts of speed for performance dogs or to get ahead of an escaping cow and to dodge hooves and horns. Dogs with poorly developed rearing muscles of the loin and back legs are not as able to leap or sprint well.

Last but Not Least - the Hind Feet

The feet are the dog's base of support. They are the part of the limb that makes contact with ground forces. It involves the manner in which the weight is distributed in the foot.

It's not possible to stress enough the importance of sound feet. During locomotion, dogs must use forces on the ground in order to bear the weight of the body and propel it forward. When the four smaller digital pads tip upward, they expose the webbing to injury similar to the splay foot. The third digital bones aren't adequately supported causing foot instability. This type of conformation is weak, causing the foot to break down from the uneven load that is placed on the joints due to laxity. **If you have _no foot_, you have _no dog_, be it for herding, hunting, search and rescue, etc.**

Some dogs need the longer metatarsi and well-developed rearing muscles of the loin, back, and legs for jumping into the air, such as Frisbee or dock-diving dogs, and even Schutzhund or police dogs that launch through a suspect's car window, take down an armed suspect, or restrain a dangerous person.

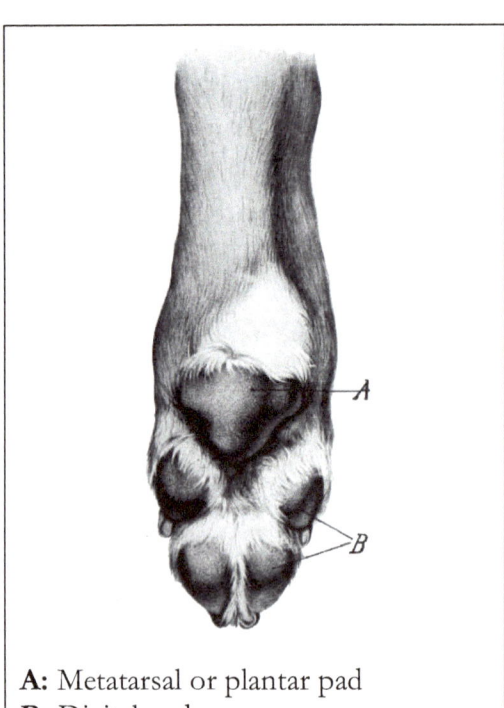

A: Metatarsal or plantar pad
B: Digital pads

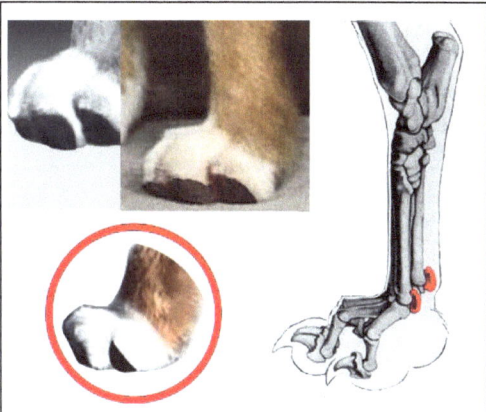

Left: Unsound feet. Right: Normal foot with sesamoid bones shown in red.

When the heart-shaped heel or plantar pads are thin and poorly developed and/or the ligaments are lax, it allows the heel to roll backward. The four smaller digital pads tip upward and shift the dog's weight on the digital sesamoid bones rather than up on the pads. The sesamoids create mechanical leverage and assist with weight bearing for tendons. Consequently, the dog's ability to absorb impact, resist tensile and compressive forces produced during muscle contractions is greatly reduced. It also exposes the webbing to injury. **This is a severe fault** since dogs need sound feet to accomplish their inherited tasks.

On the Diagonal - Going Away

In normal femoral and tibial alignment, the feet follow the line of the limb. A correctly aligned limb has its load-bearing axis on a line that goes from the hip, stifle, tarsus to the foot.

Convergence formulates from the hip joint to the feet. As the dog is trotting away from the viewer, the feet converge toward the center line of gravity, which is midpoint under the body. The dog is moving correctly when the hind limbs from the hip to paw resemble a "V" shape as the dog's legs are drawn underneath. The joints don't bend or twist when bearing weight in motion.

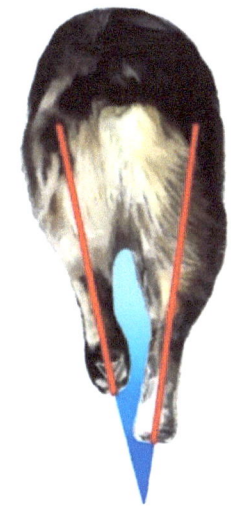

Pelvic Limb Anomalies

Bony misalignments are easy to see. The more difficult part is determining the origin. Cow hocks (inward inclination of the tarsus) is usually described as something like, "when the hocks turn in and the feet turn out." The *Encyclopedia of K-9 Terminology* by Gilbert and Gilbert defines "cow hocks" as, "When the hocks turn in, the stifle turns out and the feet toe out." Sometimes, what is perceived to be is not always the entire picture. Internal rotation of the tarsi is not always accompanied by external femoral or tibial torsion, which is what the Gilberts' assessment may be describing, "stifles turn out."

Atypical alignments are caused by musculoskeletal conditions, such as angular deformities, or rotational deformities, also known as torsion of the limbs. These can occur in one or more bones. For example, in the cuboidal bones of the tarsus and/or the long bones of the limbs.

Rotational and angular deformities affect normal range of motion, mechanical leverage and asymmetric weight bearing. Dogs with these deformities can experience uneven load distribution and affect hindlimb gait.

The anatomy of the hip also affects the normal rotation of the entire leg. In other words, the way the femoral head, the round ball, actually fits into the acetabulum (hip socket) influences how the dog's entire leg lines up with the body. For example, femoral anteversion is an inward twisting of the femur versus torsion of the femoral neck. <u>This should not be confused with the systematic rotation of the femur.</u>

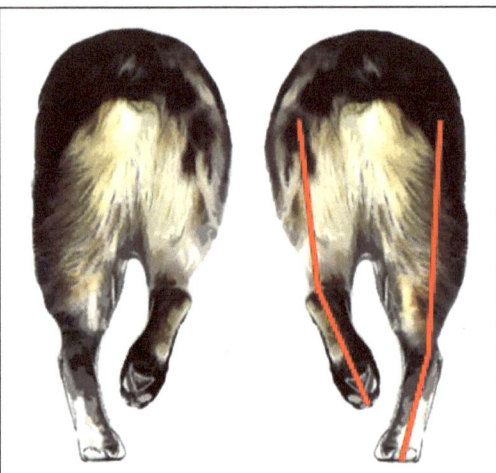

Internally rotated tarsi resulting in bowed or open hocks.

When the tarsus (hock joint) rotates outward (away from) the midline it is often referred to as bowed or "open" hocks. These bones connect to various other bones, as well as muscles, ligaments, and tendons. Femoral anteversion and tibial torsion can cause dogs to "toe in", thus reducing the power transmitted to the body.

Separating Fact from Fiction

Cow hocks are commonly tolerated in Border Collies circles, with experts stating, "They enable their dogs to get under themselves for quicker, tighter turns" or "it aids a dog in lying down and getting up quickly."

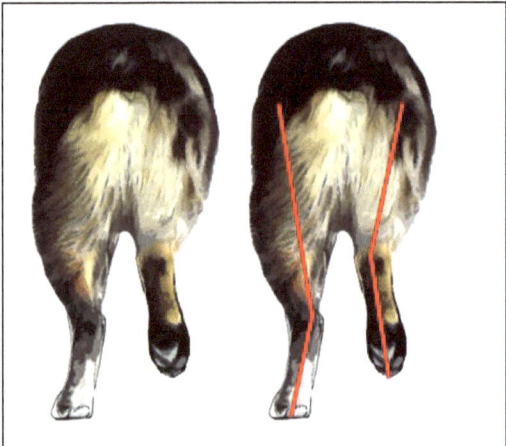

Cow hocks or externally rotated tarsi.

The crouched posture may increase torque at the tarsus, but cow hocks are **not** why they run fast and make tight turns. Cow hocks are a rotational change of the hindlimbs. They are not beneficial for repeated jumping and running over the long haul. They may continue to perform in spite of it, but this is an abnormality that causes asymmetrical wear and tear on the joint surfaces from the uneven load, which can lead to pain, injuries, and eventually arthritis.

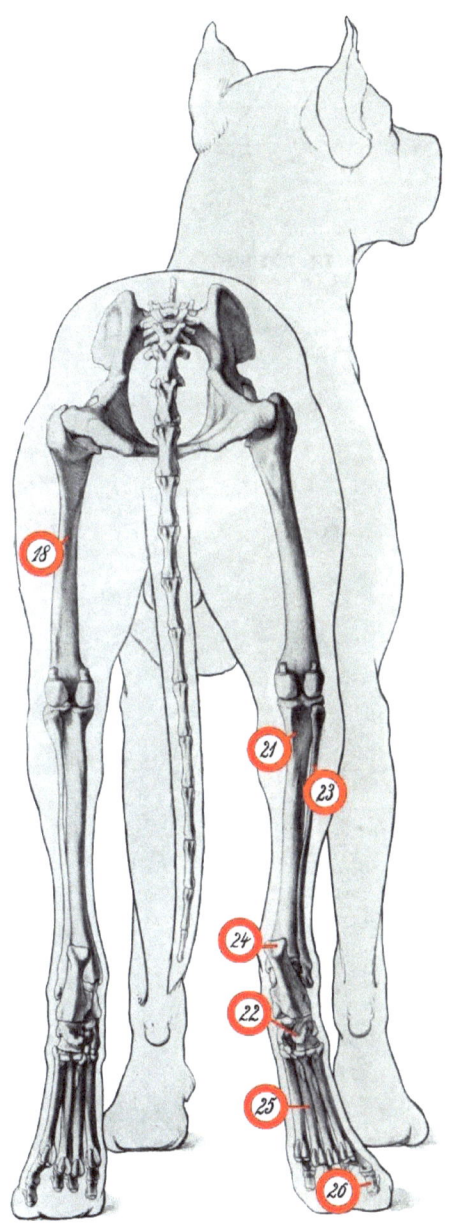
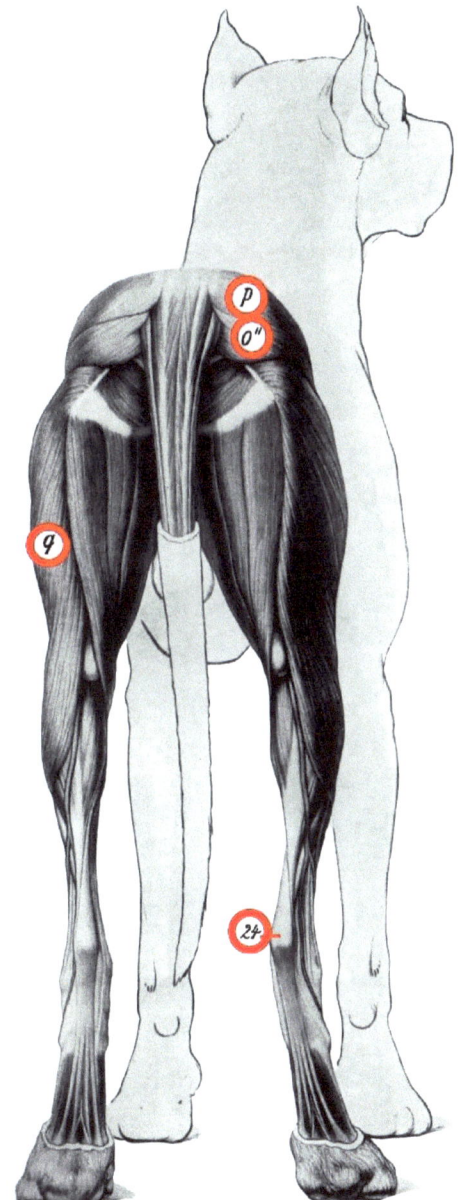

From top to bottom:

18 – Femur
21 – Tibia
22 – Tarsus
23 – Fibula
24 – Point of hock (calcaneus)
25 – Metatarsus
26 – Phalanges

From top to bottom:

p – Gluteus medius
o" – Gluteus maximus superficialis
q – Biceps femoris
24 – Point of hock

For Fun

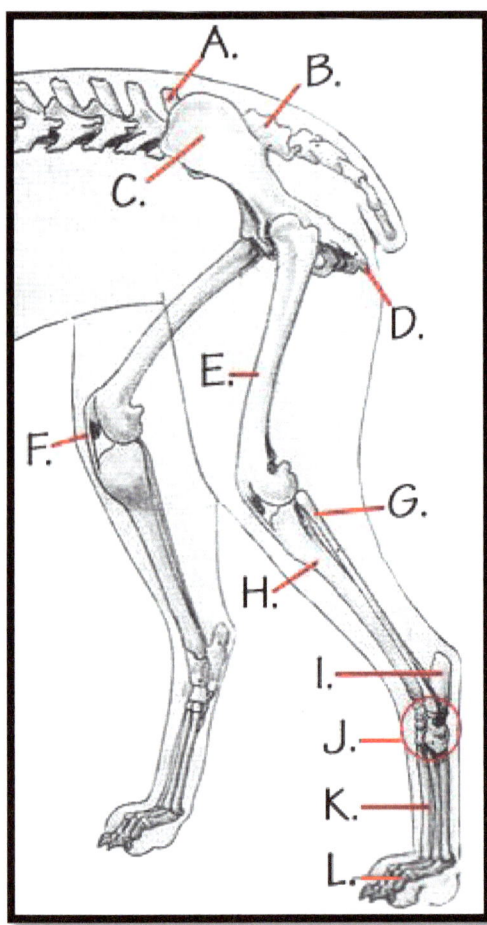

Match the anatomical parts to their corresponding letters:

Sacrum	
Ischium	
Ilium	
Patella	
Fibula	
Tibia	
Hock (tarsal) joint	
Metatarsus	
Digits	
Femur	
Calcaneus	

Can you name the underlying bones for the rear assembly?

Rump / Croup
a.
Upper thigh
b.
Lower thigh
c.
Rear pasterns
d.

Answers to Match the parts:

A. Last Lumbar Vertebrae.
B. Sacrum.
C. Ilium.
D. Ischium (point of buttock).
E. Femur.
F. Patella.
G. Fibula.
H. Tibia.
I. Calcaneus.
J. Hock (tarsal) joint.
K. Metatarsus.
L. Digits.

Answers to name the underlying bones:

a. – Pelvis (Ilium, Ischium).
b. - Femur (Upper Thigh).
c. - Tibia and Fibula (Lower Thigh).
d. - Metatarsus (Rear Pastern / Hock).

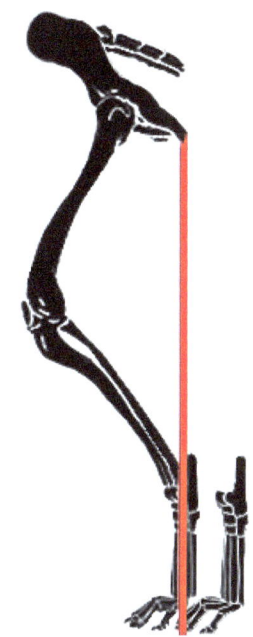

The vertical red line indicates moderate angulation. When the dog has extended angulation, its hock and foot are out behind the body and it lacks vertical support.

R. Harrison Smythe explained, "In a normal [ancestral] hind limb the force traveling to the hock after application of the hind foot to the ground, passes up the shorter tibia, which lies almost in a straight line with the femur. The force is applied from the head of the femur almost directly into the acetabulum.

"In the over-angulated limb, now in fashion," continued Smythe, "the tibia meets the lower end of the femur at an angle so that the direct drive cannot ensue and the femur can only transmit the force to the acetabulum after the rectus femoris muscle has contracted, thus enabling the femur to assume some degree of joint rigidity in its connection with the tibia."

7 The Gait

Gait is simply a way of moving. It's defined as a pattern of repetitive limb motions that a dog uses to walk, trot or gallop.

> "Dog show enthusiasts, who are oriented toward showmanship, are apt to observe exaggerated, attractive trotting styles and then mistakenly apply that exaggerated style to many breeds. Several breeds have had their functional trotting style altered into a style designed to please the [show] fancy, but not a style adapted to the breed's original function." - Curtis Brown, *Dog Locomotion and Gait Analysis*.

Balance and soundness are key in order for dogs to do their job with less fatigue and avoid injuries. Judges need to understand what is required of the herding dogs in the real world. The biggest misunderstanding about herding breeds like the Australian Shepherd, Australian Cattle Dog, or Kelpie is they are sustained trotting specialists. **This could not be further from the truth.**

On farms and ranches in the real world, Australian Shepherds, Australian Cattle Dogs, Border Collies, Kelpies and similar breeds have to negotiate uneven and sometimes rocky terrain, through heavy snow and deep sand or thick mud, which is very different than trotting across the level surface of a conformation ring.

When livestock is moved in large numbers over long distances across varied terrain, dogs are required to use all gaits from a walk to a slow jog to a trot to a flat out run. When all the animals are under control and settled, the dogs alternate from a walk to an average jog, and then may sprint to turn back any livestock that stray off the trail. This is typical of Aussies and other breeds doing this kind of work.

The angulation of the femur attachment to the pelvis must synchronize with the shoulder angulation for correct foot timing. They must be in harmony to produce a tireless gait.

Correct structure for stockdogs also means the dog can sprint and turn back runaways that have bolted from the herd. Dogs that compete in the sport of agility need the ability to stop, turn and make abrupt changes in directions.

During the sprint, there are instances when only one of the dog's feet touch the ground. When this happens, every now and then, the dog's body is being driven entirely by the energy already in motion.

Length of stride is measured from the place where one paw leaves the ground to the place where the same paw again strikes the ground. The length of stride and the timing of the footfall correspond with speed and agility. "A dog that takes long steps will have its legs stretched further forward and rearward, which slows turning due to centrifugal forces produced by the extended limbs.

"Ideally a dog should have its feet under the body when turning to reduce the amount of mass that is further from the center of rotation. This decreases centrifugal force, making it easier to turn.

"Having a higher stride frequency (shorter gait cycle) and the ability to change direction quickly has also been observed in horses and cheetahs." - *Quantitative Comparison of the Walk and Trot of Border Collies and Labrador Retrievers, Breeds with Different Performance Requirements* - Carr BJ, Canapp SO Jr, and Zink MC.

Agile dogs swivel or pivot from the center line, rather than pulling themselves around. A balanced gait translates to athletic ability.

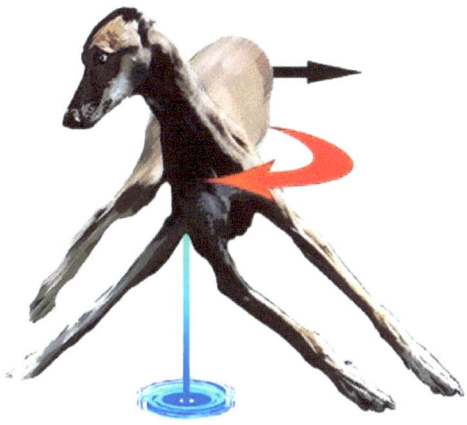

Turning off the centerline, the dog's momentum is going one direction as indicated above by the black arrow. In order to turn 90- or 180-degrees mid-stride, the dog must pivot off the centerline (blue) and in the next stride sprint in the direction it just came from (red).

An example of Aussies pivoting off the centerline to change directions in the middle of a stride.

Pivoting off the centerline is key for dogs to excel in dog sports like Agility.

The Trot

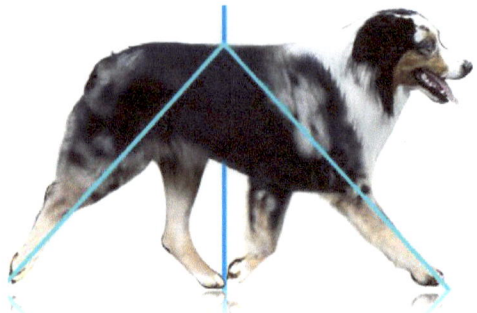

Dogs should be gaited on a loose lead because a tight lead:

- Puts pressure on the neck causing the dog to lift its front feet upward rather than forward.
- Can cause the appearance of gaiting faults when none exist.
- Hinders a dog from shifting its center of gravity forward.

In the trot, there are only two feet on the ground at any given time. Dogs are judged at the trot because it's where all forces are, or should be, in balance. It is easier to see the:

- Interplay between the fore-and hind-assemblies
- Topline
- Foot timing / foot fall
- Abnormal gait, determining causes and location of lameness.

Gait Cycles and Foot Timing of the Trot

Gait cycles can be broken down into two primary phases, the **stance**, or vaulting, phase (weight bearing), and the **swing** (non-weight bearing) phase. In the stance phase, the dog is "vaulted" over the stationary front foot to give rise, drive, and fall. The opposite forelimb that was in the swing phase takes over support and power. This frees the foot that was in stance phase to enter the swing phase. In the swing phase, the foot is lifted, quickly carried forward in extension and then smoothly retracted as the pad impact takes place, thus completing that gait cycle.

A dog's femur and opposite scapula are matching motion in a diagonal gait.

The rearlimb impacts first with a very close concurrent retraction of the forepad. Both front feet and hind feet are synced to the weight-bearing foot. The front weight-bearing foot leaves the ground a split-second before the hind foot "fills" its imprint. That is to say, the hind foot should step into the print left by the front foot.

As the metacarpal (palmar) pad impacts the ground, the action carries the weight load forward from the plantar pad to the digital pads of the toes, the pastern is simultaneously flexing to absorb shock. The scapula and diagonal femur are also in coordinated motion.

The degree of propulsion is fairly evenly divided between the fore- and hind-limbs. Some dogs use a skip step, an intermittent hop, in the rhythm of the trot when transitioning from a walk (four beat gait) to a trot (two beat gait).

The gait will be **balanced** when the angulation of the front assembly complements the angulation of the hindquarters and there is flawless coordination between the supporting and propelling ends of the body.

leading front foot as it contacts the ground. As a result, the corresponding hind foot would reach its full extension in the backward stroke. In the process of carrying the body forward over the forepaw, the muscles contract to shorten and lengthen the limbs.

The picture above is a view of the wolf's thoracic, weight-bearing foot leaving the ground, as the hind foot moves into position to "fill" its place. Pay attention to your dog's natural head carriage during the trotting gait off-lead.

As the thoracic weight-bearing front foot leaves the ground, the hind foot moves into position to "fill" its place (as pictured bottom left column). The next photo frame would catch the

The front leg of the dog pictured above is positioned to strike the ground at a moderate angle, which is easier on the joints over long distances than a dog with more angulation.

Don't mistake a normal, level head carriage for a dog that continually travels with its head down shifting weight--adjusting the amount of weight that it puts on a limb due to an injury or pain and discomfort. Dogs that have lower than level head and neck carriage due to weak muscling move arduously. It's not light and agile, but heavy.

The forward and rearward extensions are balanced one to the other. In other words, the forward reach equals the backstroke (backward reach). The pelvic limb or hind leg follows through on the back stroke giving the rear legs adequate backward thrust.

wolves, and other members of the canine family.

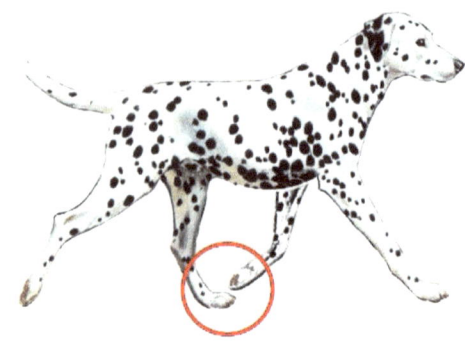

The forelimb should not only reach forward but reach back freely. In other words, the joints are not limited in their ability to flex and extend as needed in the stance and swing phases.

Choppy gait is caused by an imbalance. The thoracic limbs are not in unity with the pelvic limbs. There's a little more balance in the image above than the dog pictured below because the dog below lacks balance.

In the instant of time pictured above, the lifted right rear foot has shifted the load to the supporting left front foot. The weight center is moving forward, and to the right of the under support. At the same time, a right-forward diagonal change is taking place. The left rear will impact next, followed by the right front.

Balanced Trot

It's important to know what is considered normal in order to recognize abnormal. In the balanced trot, the hind foot fills the imprint left by the front foot. This includes dogs,

Over-Driving

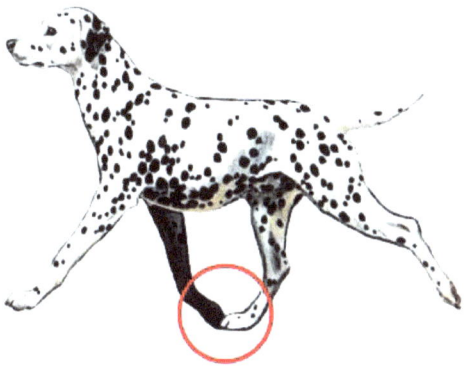

Over-driving causes the hind foot to reach beyond (overreach) the front footprint. The front foot is still on the ground rather than lifted out of the way when the hind foot hits the ground.

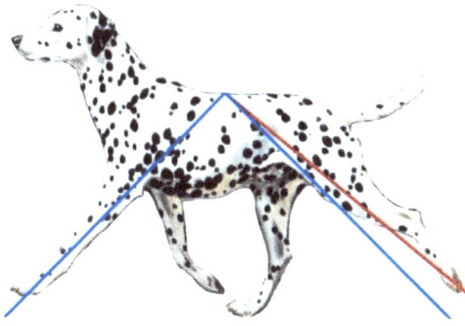

One of the most common things you see in the show-ring today is over-angulation. The extra kick out behind is inefficient motion.

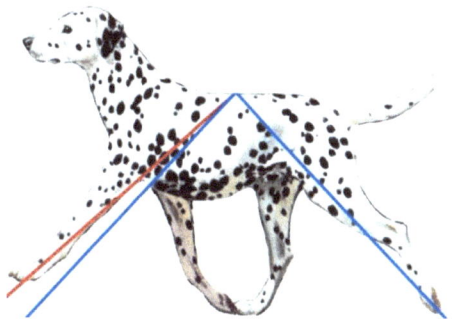

So too is padding (above) which is a delayed action that occurs to prevent interference when the hindquarters overdrive the forequarters.

When the hind foot overreaches the front foot, problems, such as crabbing, twisting the spine, and padding (also known as dwelling) result due to more angulation and drive from behind than from in front. To avoid this problem, some breeders perpetuate long-bodied dogs. That way the feet won't interfere when trotting in the show ring.

It is not over-driving (hind paw steps beyond the fore-print) when a dog is turning to change directions, such as moving laterally behind livestock (above). Yet again, notice each dog's natural head carriage while working above and below.

Evaluating gaits - the smoothness or roughness of a gait - takes practice. You can become proficient at gait analysis by observing dogs in action. For example, study the pattern of footsteps by gaiting the dog on the beach or through a thin layer of wet snow or sand. You can also paint the dog's pads with glycerin, which is safe, and gait the dog across smooth, dry pavement.

Side Note: Soundness

In all the years we worked Australian Shepherds in difficult and diverse conditions, I cannot recall the type of injuries, such as torn or ruptured CCL (cranial cruciate ligament), also known as an ACL (anterior cruciate ligament), that seem so common today. Our dogs experienced sudden twisting motions on unstable surfaces, and I attribute lack of injuries to the fact that they were structurally sound and moderate in every aspect.

ACL type injuries are hardly ever seen in sled dogs. According to Stuart Nelson Jr., DVM, chief veterinarian of the Iditarod International Sled Dog Race, "Fortunately, CrCL injuries are rare in sled dogs. Many factors can explain this, including good conformation, proper condition and hybrid vigor. When it does occur, it is usually the result of an acute incident, such as stepping in a hole and/or hyperextension of the joint"

Separating Fact from Fiction

People have gotten so used to seeing over angulated dogs in the conformation ring they don't recognize the moderate, normal angulation of working and performance dogs.

Long tibias that place the feet out behind the body produce marked angulation. The tibia articulates with the femur at an abnormal angle which places strain on the cranial cruciate ligament and therefore more vulnerable to injury.

The picture above is an excellent example of a moderate, balanced Aussie. This dog lived a long healthy life. He was an athletic working dog and never had any health or <u>soundness</u> issues. Notice the metatarsal pads line up beneath the ischium for maximum turn-around efficiency. Also, there's a vertical line of support from the upper midpoint of the dog's shoulder to the metacarpal (palmar) pad.

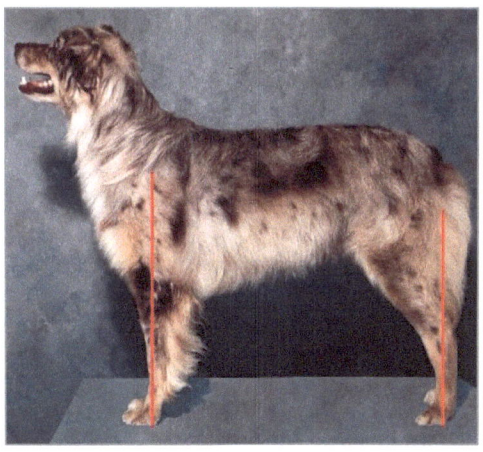

Unfortunately, people have been led to believe a normal stifle is a "straight stifle." Nothing could be further from the truth.

Detecting Problems

If a dog is standing and the weight is not shared by the other limbs, it could indicate a problem. If a dog drops its head toward the ground (cranially) to shift weight while gaiting, it may indicate pain or structural weakness in the front end. Lameness in the front end tends to cause dogs to shift their weight caudally (toward the rear) and drop their heads down on the sound forelimb.

Dogs with shoulder lameness may move with shorter strides. Dogs with lameness in the hindquarters tend to shift their weight cranially (toward the head). They have a tendency to extend their head and neck to offset weight from the hind end.

Every now and then, dogs will stand with their metatarsal pads placed nearer to the hip joint instead of under the point of buttock. This is **not** a problem <u>unless</u> the ligaments of the hocks don't allow full extension in the back swing, thus limiting rear leg extension. In that case, it would be known as sickle hocks and would impede or limit the dog's athletic ability.

Sometimes a dog with nice conformation - seemingly sound thoracic and pelvic limbs - can exhibit gaiting irregularities. Three things that cause instability are:

1. Pain from degenerative joint problems, such as osteoarthritis
2. Abnormal hip joints or hip dysplasia
3. Ligament damage or laxity, such as "slipped hocks" (the joint hyperextends/bends forward).

A hitch (skip step in a hind leg) in the gait, however, can be due to a patellar luxation (PL), also known as luxating patella or floating patella. If the groove at the end of the femur (trochlea) is too shallow, the patella may slip out of position. Angular limb anomalies of the long bones also change the ergonomics of the stifle joint. PL is one of the most common hindlimb orthopedic pathologies seen in small dogs. It occurs in other animals, as well.

Muscle tremors

Involuntary muscle movements in the hind legs are not a matter of structural deficiencies, but a problem with the dog's nervous system controlling the limbs. Trembling can be caused by viral, toxic substances, or dietary imbalances, in some cases.

Muscle tremors differ from the temporary quivering caused by excitement, for example, when a dog is about to start an agility run. What I'm referring to are the muscle tremors caused by an underlying neurological disorder, such as hypomyelinogenesis. In this condition, there is a lack of myelination, mainly in the spinal cord, but also in parts of the brain. Myelin is the fatty substance that provides protection and a pathway for cellular transmissions in the normal nerve signals.

It has been proven to be a genetic disease in certain breeds. The frequency with which it's seen in breeds like the Australian Shepherd suggests it's hereditary. <u>Working dogs require nerves of steel,</u> not feebleness.

Rolling Across the Topline

Just beneath the skin's surface is a mesh of loose connective tissue called fascia, a unique architectural system made up of collagen fibers that literally forms the body. It connects the skin to the tissues that are directly beneath it. Superficial fascia carries major blood vessels, nerves, and lymphatic channels. Fascia also stores fat and water, and has nerve receptors that make it almost as sensitive as skin. In addition, fascia acts as a shock absorbing cushion and helps protect underlying tissues from injury caused by bumps and blows to the body surface.

Genetics and the spongy nature of the subcutaneous tissue determines the relative mobility of the skin. Dogs with skin that rolls have loosely woven connective tissue. It doesn't snap back as efficiently as dogs with a more resilient constitution. It is **not** the same as dogs that have poor muscle tone (soft and flabby) from a lack of fitness.

The Pace

In contrast to the trot where diagonal support makes it easy to maintain equilibrium, the pace is a two-beat lateral gait in which the front and hind legs on the same side of the body move in tandem. The center of gravity shifts from side-to-side. It's often referred to as a fatigue gait and occurs at speeds between a walk and a trot.

It's thought that puppies in some bloodlines in some breeds pace until their muscles are better developed. But there's also a genetic component to pacing.

Pacing is not uncommon in short bodied dogs like the Old English Sheepdog with a higher center of gravity. The breed's standard states, "Very elastic at a gallop. May amble or pace at slower speeds."

Don't mistake the amble (a transitional gait between the walk and a trot) for the pace. Some people are unable to walk quickly enough to keep up with their dogs and hinder them from being able to transition into a trot.

Pacing is **not** an efficient gait for agility. Dogs that pace **cannot** break into a sprint easily and are not in a position to shift off the centerline, as when making a 90- or 180-degree turn. Their thoracic and pelvic limbs impact the ground beside the centerline, not on it.

Separating Fact from Fiction

It has been suggested that pacing is a fatigue gait or it is used when dogs experience discomfort from an injury or if their muscles are sore after a long walk in the park.

In 2016, the authors of *Evaluation of pacing as an indicator of musculoskeletal pathology in dogs* stated, "Little is currently known about the pacing gait in dogs and it has been speculated that pacing may be utilized by dogs with musculoskeletal pathology." The goals of their research were to determine if pacing in dogs is associated with musculoskeletal disease. They also wanted to establish if controlled speed impacts pacing. Dogs underwent orthopedic and lameness assessments. In summary, "Pacing should be considered a gait variation that can be observed in clinically normal dogs at speeds between walk and trot."

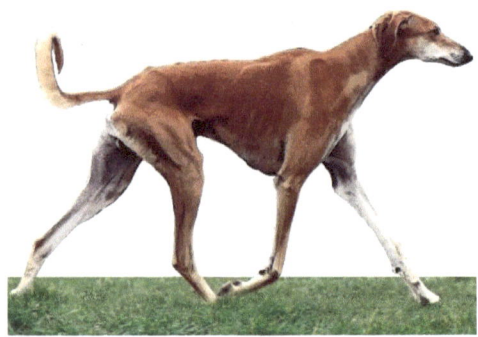

The dog's ability to walk and run is dependent on a complex coordination of muscle contractions carried out by nerve cells called motor neurons in their spinal cord. These networks produce left–right alternation of limbs as well as coordinated activation of flexor and extensor muscles.

In dogs, as well as horses, observations have been made that suggest pacing is likely to be influenced by genes in the physiology of the skeletal muscle and nervous system.

Enter the Gait Keeper Gene

The American Standardbred horse is well known for its trotting and pacing ability. They are subdivided into two groups, pacers and trotters. They have the ability to trot or pace at high speed without breaking into a gallop, the natural gait at high speed for horses. Maintaining a trot at high speeds without breaking into a gallop is a critical component of harness racing.

In 2012, scientists in Sweden discovered a single gene mutation in DMRT3, originally called "**Loss of Canter.**" This *Gait Keeper* gene influences the pattern of locomotion—a horse's ability to trot or pace. It encodes a transcription factor involved in the coordination of the locomotor system in vertebrates and is responsible for synchronizing the left and right sides of the horse's body and is associated with racing performance. This genetic variant can be a limiting factor for the development of faster sprinting ability because it causes significant changes in the motor coordination for trotting and sprinting. Carriers find it hard to transition from trotting or pacing to sprinting. They lack the necessary coordination. DMRT3 gene mutations are almost non-existent in the wild populations.

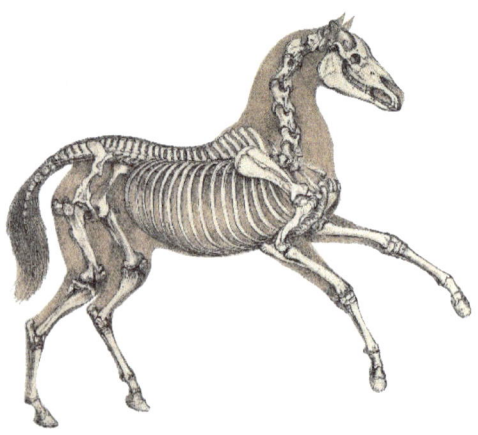

"Humans have spread this mutation across the world primarily because horses carrying this mutation are able to provide a very smooth ride," said Leif Andersson, PhD, researcher at Uppsala University and the Swedish University of Agricultural Sciences.

Dr. Andersson stated, "It seems that besides enabling ambling and pacing, this Gait Keeper gene seems to also inhibit transition from the trot to the gallop."

The term gallop is essentially an umbrella word for various running gaits including the sprint. In the horse world, the slow gallop is often referred to as the canter.

"Horses lose their sprinting power because of the special muscle type that enables explosive speed over a short time." - Laura Bas Conn, a veterinarian MsC at the Department for Animal Breeding and Genetics at the Swedish University of Agricultural Science.

Locomotion results from an interplay between biomechanical constraints of the muscles attached to the skeleton and the neuronal circuits controlling and coordinating muscle activities. "Locomotion in mammals relies on a central pattern-generating circuitry of spinal interneurons established during development that coordinates limb movement. These networks produce left-right alternation of limbs as well as coordinated activation of flexor and extensor muscles." – *Mutations in DMRT3 affect locomotion in horses and spinal circuit function in mice,* L. Andersson, M. Larhammar, K. Kullander

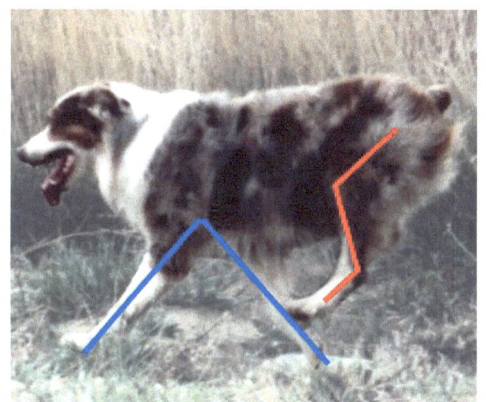

An Aussie with a sprinting drivetrain transitioning from a trot (marked by blue) to a sprint (marked by red) in midair.

Experiments on this gene in mice have led to fundamental new knowledge about the neural circuits that control leg movements. The study is a breakthrough for our understanding of spinal cord neuronal circuitry and its control of locomotion in vertebrates. "Mice with a mutation in DMRT3 are extremely interesting - they have great difficulty coordinating their legs at all. That is partly how it was determined that the DMRT3 mutation is involved in limb coordination, and in horses it appears that the mutation allows partial 'loosening' of the strict 'coordination rules,' so that it is possible for horses to perform other gaits that aren't in the 'normal' pattern. However, the mutation is not severe enough that it completely gets rid of the ability to coordinate the limbs." – Dr. Melissa L. Cox, Center for Animal Genetics

"It is truly great when this type of interdisciplinary collaboration results in such ground breaking discoveries. There was no information in the scientific literature on the function of the DMRT3 prior to the publication of our article. This protein is present in all vertebrates for which data are available, and it is likely that DMRT3 nerve cells have a central role for coordinating movements in humans as well," Klas Kullander concluded. - *Single Gene Has Major Impact on Gaits in Horses and in Mice.*

An English Shepherd exhibiting tremendous reach and drive during this trot without breaking gait.

Genomic methods under development for navigating mouse and human genomes are readily transferable to studying the dog genome. Although a test is currently not available to identify the gait mutation in dogs, I believe there's a strong genetic component for dogs with a propensity for pacing and those dogs that are able to trot without breaking gait. People are selecting for it without even realizing it because conformation show dogs are highly prized for their trotting style.

Side Note: In all the years my family bred, trained, and worked the Las Rocosa line of Australian Shepherds, I never saw any of those Aussies pace. There would have been plenty of opportunities for them to experience discomfort and sore muscles during spring or fall roundups when the dogs were worked day in and day out.

I have taught stockdog clinics across North America and in Europe with dogs that were unable to outmaneuver the livestock. Not because they were disinterested, but because they had difficulty making the transition from a trot to a sprint.

My parents were lifelong learners. They had a great eye for conformation and gait in both horses and dogs. The functional changes Dad identified in Australian Shepherds is what I believe to be a change in the physiology of the skeletal muscle and nervous system.

 **From the Desk of Steve Shope**

The first time I met Ernie Hartnagle was in the early 90s at his home in Boulder, Colorado. I had made the trip from New Mexico to try and get a dog from their kennel. I had had several Aussies that were just farm dogs that were not registered in the past. I had become interested in trialing and was looking for a registered dog to compete in the ASCA stockdog trials with. I knew that the Hartnagles were long time, trusted breeders thus my trip.

When I arrived, Ernie was working a little red Aussie bitch that was a real spitfire and I was mesmerized with her instinct and ability to control and work the sheep. She looked like a little Quarter Horse bred to cut.

I had a pleasant conversation with Ernie that afternoon as we talked about working dogs and how instinct and structure played a significant role in their success and usefulness. They didn't have any dogs available at the time. Little did I know that this was the beginning of the friendship with the whole Hartnagle family.

Ernie Hartnagle measuring an Australian Shepherd at 78 years of age

Ernie and I developed a relationship as the mentor and student. You just had to listen: he already had a lifetime of wisdom and experience earned by trial and error. We had many conversations about breeding objectives both from the point of view of structure, instinct and health. Ernie really believed all three were important for a breed to be successful. Breeders needed to work on all three.

As we discussed movement associated with a dog's agility and movement when controlling livestock, he pointed out how important it was for a dog to be able to work off their rear ends. The ability to pivot right and left with a minimum effort in changing direction. When you are loading a trailer or working chutes, this ability to work off their backend readily becomes apparent while holding pressure and covering the livestock. This ability also helps the dog get out of the way when needed to avoid injury. I have found that they are the more instinctive dogs, as well.

He emphasized that good structure is related to a dog's ability to conserve energy-- probably going back to when they had to hunt for themselves. Hunting consumed a lot of energy and poor hunters didn't survive. I have personally found this to be true in my past and present dogs.

Ernie often would compare what he saw and valued in a good using horse to the same characteristics he saw in his best working dogs.

8 The Head

Perhaps no other single factor sets one breed apart from other breeds and contributes as strongly to breed identification as does the head. This feature also distinguishes major bloodlines within the breed.

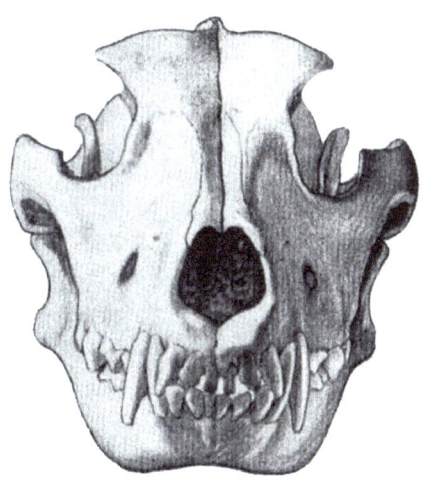

The skull is the framework of the head and houses the brain, dentition, ears, eyes, and nose (sinus chambers). The structure protects and minimizes the effects of injury to the brain including the special senses - sight, hearing, and scent. The formation and depth of the sinus chambers (the stop) adds structural stability to the frame without adding extra weight, which is important in respiration.

Heads are classified as the mesocephalic or normal form of the ancestral dog as seen in wolves, as well as the Beauceron, Australian Shepherd, and German Shepherd Dog.

Dolichocephalic is the elongated face with the extended cranium, as seen in the Collie, Greyhound, and Saluki.

And lastly, the short-faced brachycephalic breeds of dogs like Boxers, Bulldogs, and even short-muzzled Rottweilers. Dogs with short faces can have a number of craniofacial anomalies "including a reduction in the length of bones that form the rostrum, chondrodysplasia of the cranial base, and changes in the palate position relative to the cranial base." – *The*

Genetics of Canine Skull Shape Variation –
Schoenebeck and Ostrander

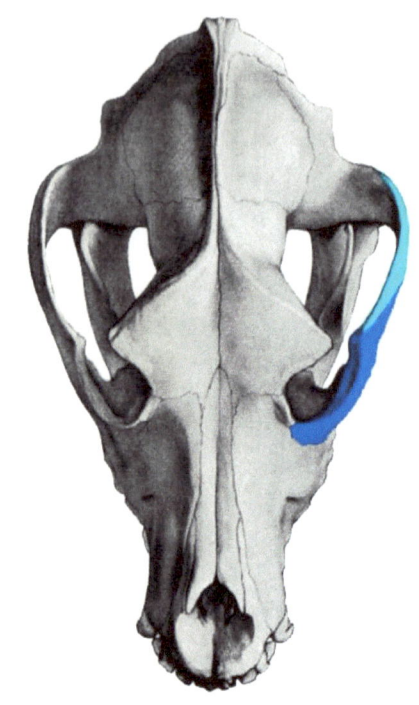

Heads are divided into two parts: the foreface, also known as the front portion of the skull (yellow), and the cranium, also referred to as the topskull (in red).

The frontal process of the zygomatic bone is highlighted in dark blue, and the zygomatic process of the temporal bone, the zygomatic arch or cheekbone, is highlighted in cyan.

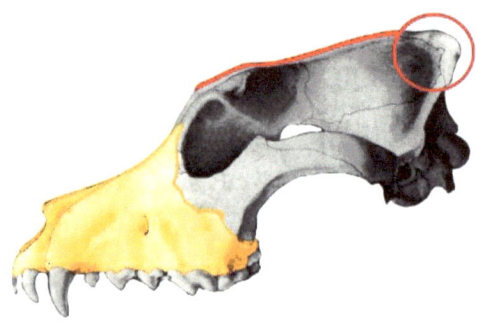

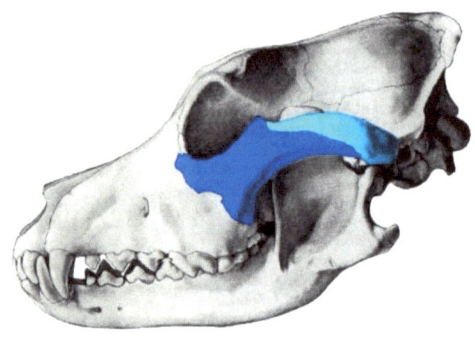

The ridge of bone along the topskull is the sagittal crest indicated by the reddish line (above). The sagittal crest on the top skull allows for the attachment of muscles used for biting. It further affords protection from a blow to the top of the head. The upper, caudal most extremity of the topskull is the occipital crest, also called the median nuchal line, as circled above.

The orbit, or eye socket, connects directly with the zygomatic arch. The arch is formed from parts of both the zygomatic bone and the temporal bone. The extension of the temporal bone is known as the zygomatic process. Depending on the degree of development and width of the zygomatic arch into which the upper edge of the masseter muscle is inserted, the dog will contribute to the shape of the cheek.

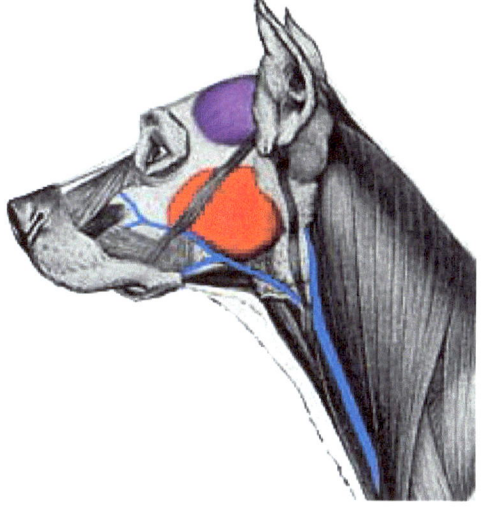

The mandible or lower jaw requires large and powerful muscles whose attachments occupy large areas of the skull surface and the zygomatic arch. The temporal muscles (purple) and masseter muscles (red) are attached to the side of the zygomatic bone.

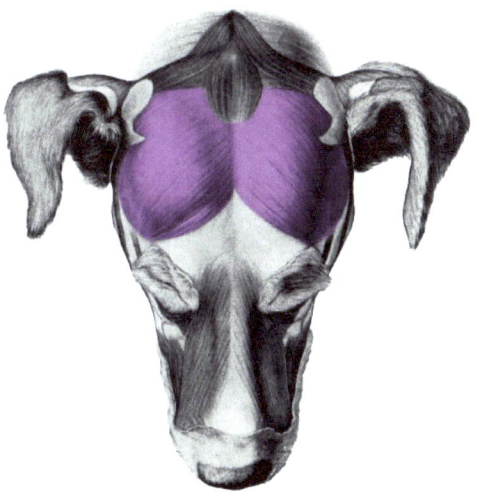

The temporal fossa (shallow depression) on either side of the sagittal crest is where the temporal muscles lodge. The temporal muscle

(highlighted in purple) is the largest muscle of the head. It's also a major retractor of the mandible or lower jaw.

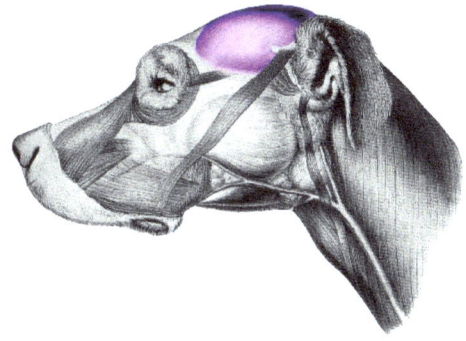

A lateral view of the structures of the head that are deeper than the superficial muscles (pictured above).

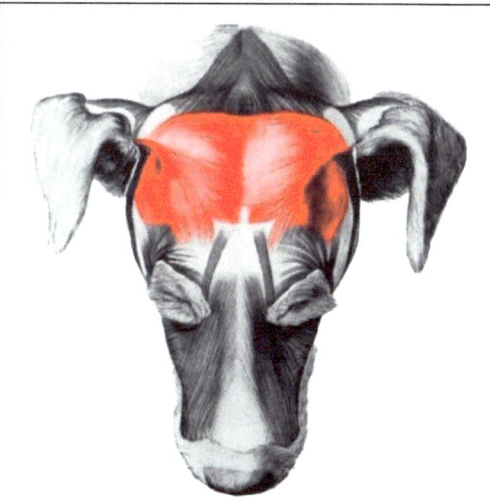

The superficial muscles of the head and the common muscle of the ear that lie in the subcutaneous tissues.

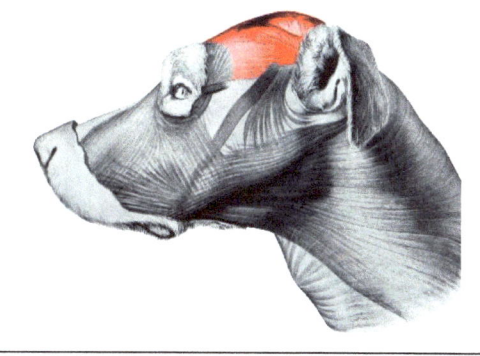

Temporomandibular Joint - TMJ

The temporomandibular joint hinges the mandible (lower jaw) to the skull. The mandible essentially pivots between the open and closed positions from the temporomandibular joint. It has a substantial influence on the bite because teeth dictate its function.

An injury to the temporomandibular joint is usually referred to as TMJ. However, that said, developmental problems can limit range of motion, making it more difficult, as well as painful, for the dog to open and close its mouth to drink, eat or pick up items, such as a toy or ball.

The Teeth

Digestion begins with the teeth. That's why the bite is considered part of the digestive system. Dogs with a malocclusion - abnormal bite or misaligned teeth - are not able to chew food into fine enough particles for proper digestion, which will affect their overall health and stamina.

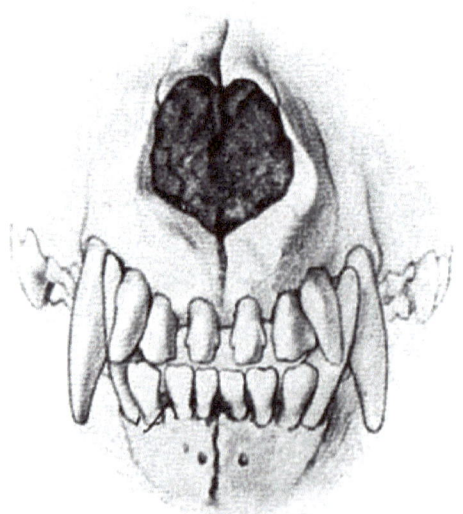

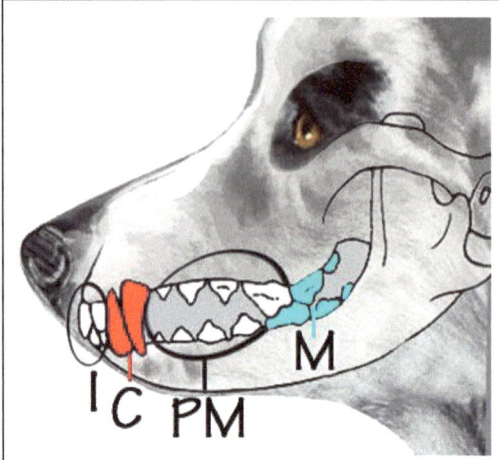

Teeth: I: Incisors, **C:** Canines, **PM:** Premolars, **M:** Molars.

The illustration above explains a full complement of 42 teeth that meet in a scissors bite. The top, or maxillary, has six incisors (central, intermediate, and corner), two canine teeth, eight premolars, and four molars. The bottom, or mandible, is exactly the same plus it has two additional molars.

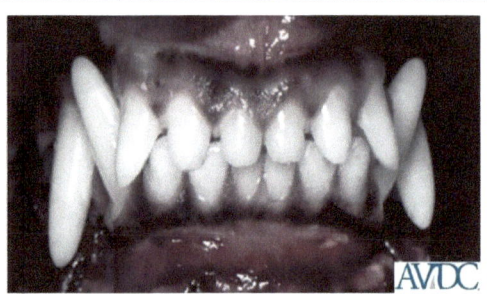

Pictured above is a normal interplay between the top and bottom central incisors and the outer canine teeth.

Each type of tooth has a very specific function. The incisors (located at the center of each dental arch) are vitally important for picking up food, removing burrs and the like from foot pads and the coat, cutting umbilical cords during the whelping process, and many other tasks.

Dogs have four deeply rooted canine teeth (cuspids): two in the upper (maxillary) and two in the lower (mandibular) arch. They are larger than incisors and used for tearing and puncturing. The premolars (bicuspids) have two points for shearing and shredding, and the large molars are for grinding and crushing.

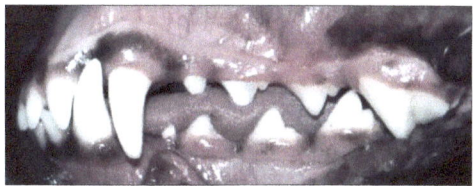

The scissors bite is anatomically correct and the most functional bite for dogs. It's indicative of a sound jaw assembly. The scissors bite lends substance and support to the face and dentition.

The scissors bite also enables the herding dog to "grip" livestock with a pinching effect and be able to withstand the impact if kicked while working.

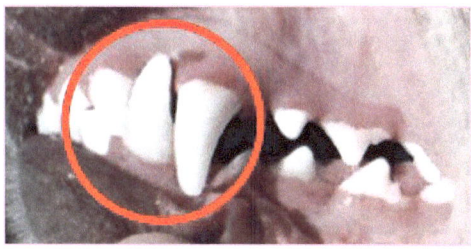

A normal scissors bite cannot be accurately judged by examining the incisors alone. The incisors can shift through trauma or surgery. The relationship of the canine or "fang" teeth—how they meet—is one good reference point for determining if the bite is correct.

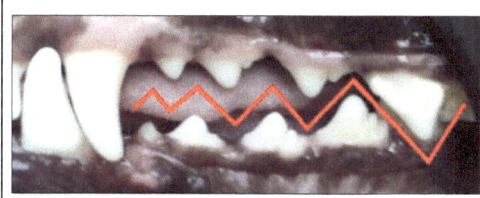

When viewed from the side—the upper and lower premolars should interdigitate; that is, the lower first premolar sits in front of the upper first premolar, and the rest of the upper and lower premolars alternate in sawtooth fashion. Overall, the premolars should give the appearance of pinking shear scissors.

Skull Alignment

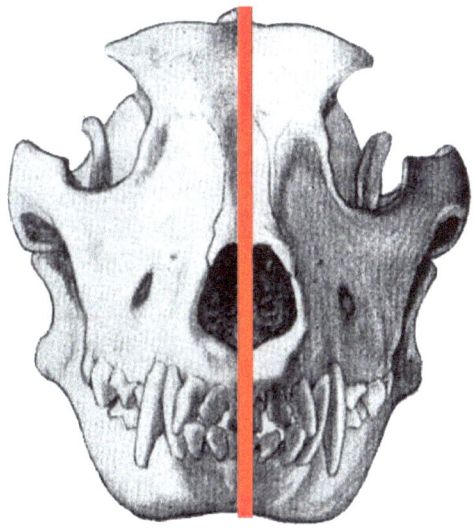

The midline of the head, starting with the occipital crest (top/back point of the skull), as well as the midpoint between the eyes, the midline of the nose pad, and the midline of both the upper and lower arches, should lie on the same plane (in a straight line) as illustrated above.

Maxillomandibular Asymmetry

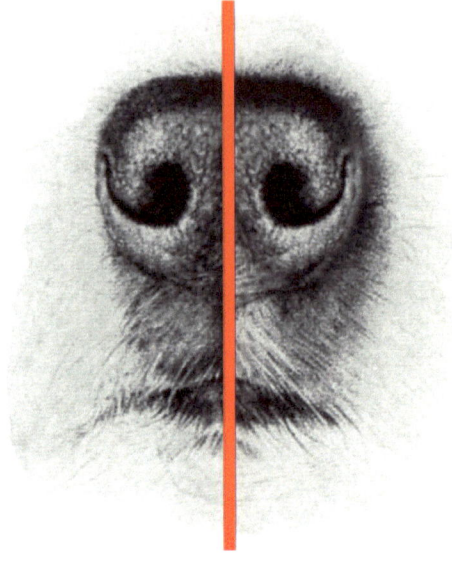

"Asymmetry may occur in the upper and or lower jaws. When there is a length disparity between the right and left side it is referred to as a rostrocaudal asymmetry (upper and/or lower). When the asymmetry results in a lack of centering of the upper and lower jaws over each other causing midline shift, then it is referred to as a side-to-side asymmetry. Finally, there may be an asymmetry that is exhibited as an abnormal (increased) space between the upper and lower jaws (may affect one or both sides) and is referred to as an open bite."- Lorraine Hiscox DVM FAVD Dip. AVDC; Jan Bellows, DVM, Dipl. AVDC, ABV- *Malocclusions in Dogs – When Teeth Are Malaligned.*

Skeletal and Dental Malocclusions

There are two types of abnormal tooth alignments: Dental malposition and skeletal malocclusion. A dental malposition occurs when the upper and lower jaw lengths are considered normal but there may be one or more teeth that are out of normal alignment. A skeletal malocclusion results when an abnormal jaw length creates a malalignment of the teeth. According to the Sacramento Veterinary Dental Services, "When malocclusions are caused by skeletal deformity and abnormal jaw length, this is considered genetic and affected animals should not be bred."

Malocclusions can be a problem if they cause abnormal tooth-to-tooth or tooth-to-soft tissue contact. They can cause pain and dysfunction. When a dental or skeletal malocclusion causes trauma to other teeth or to the oral soft tissues, the condition is termed non-functional or traumatic.

Overshot Bite

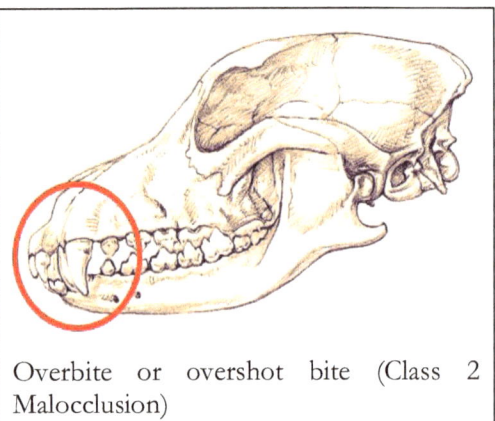

Overbite or overshot bite (Class 2 Malocclusion)

The overshot/overbite (mandibular brachygnathism), commonly called parrot mouth, occurs when the lower jaw (mandible) is relatively short compared to the upper jaw (maxilla). This conformation fault positions the lower premolars and molars behind the normal point, ultimately affecting the dog's overall health and condition. An overbite makes it difficult for puppies to suck and chew and for adult dogs to efficiently and comfortably chew and leaves the upper teeth more exposed to trauma. It can also cause considerable pain when the lower incisors hit the palate.

During the growth phase the mouth may become "slightly" overshot until the mandible catches up to the maxilla. When this occurs in a puppy (at approximately five or six months) that previously exhibited a normal scissors bite it is more than likely a temporary condition.

Even or Level Bite

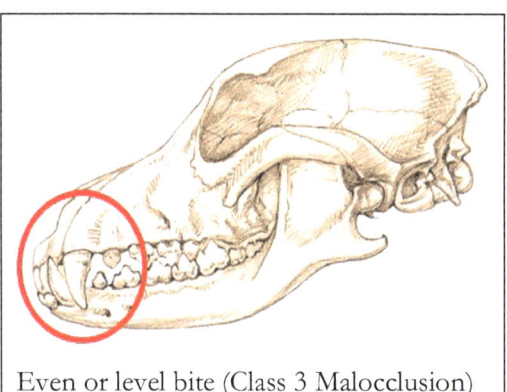

Even or level bite (Class 3 Malocclusion)

When the maxilla is shorter than the mandible, the bite is known as a level bite. The incisors meet edge to edge. The interplay between the lower canine tooth and outermost upper incisor and between the upper canine tooth and the lower and upper premolar cusp tips are all affected, according to the degree of shift. The more the bottom jaw shifts forward, the greater the tendency toward occlusal trauma (broken, chipped, abnormal and unevenly worn teeth). The excessive and uneven wear on the upper and lower incisors erodes the teeth during normal chewing, eventually, eventually creating a host of issues. Poor bites can affect the overall health of the dog and cause pain and discomfort.

The forward position of the jaw leaves the mandible more prone to injury because it is less protected. The mandible is more vulnerable because it attaches to the head in only one place. Therefore, the force cannot be dispersed when the mandible is subjected to trauma.

The level bite is undesirable because it's a genetically abnormal occlusion. A number of breed standards allow for level bites. But what's acceptable in a breed standard and what is truly healthy for the breed is sometimes in disagreement. Furthermore, according to the American Veterinary Dental Association (AVDA) the level bite is a class 3 mandibular prognathism and considered an abnormal occlusion. This can lead to abnormal wear as well as periodontal disease.

Underbite

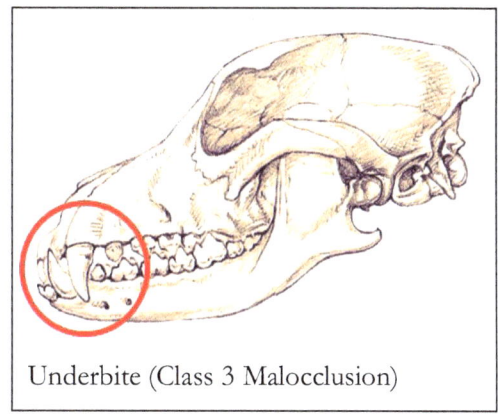

Underbite (Class 3 Malocclusion)

An underbite (mandibular prognathism), sometimes referred to as a reverse scissors bite, occurs when the upper jaw is too short (maxillary brachygnathism) causing the lower jaw to protrude beyond the upper jaw (maxilla) causing the lower incisors to overlap the top incisors, resulting in total malalignment of all the teeth. Underbites have similar problems as the level bite, but in more extreme ways including pain. The short upper jaw often results in crowded and rotated teeth, which can cause abnormal wear as well as periodontal disease.

Wry Bite

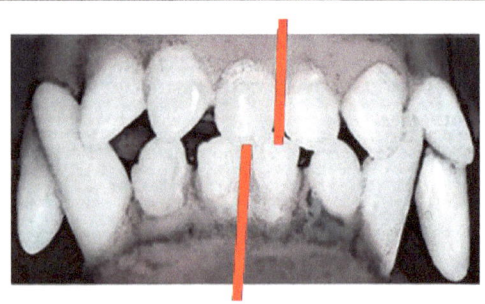

Wry Bite (Class 4 Malocclusion). The lines on the picture above should meet rather than being offset.

Wry bite is a lay term for an asymmetrical bite. One side of the jaw grows longer than the other, sometimes causing an "open bite" where their teeth are unable to fit together normally. This is considered a genetic problem, but may be caused by trauma as the jaws are growing, leading to different growth rates of the jaw.

Loss of Contact of Center Incisors

Loss of contact by center incisors is not an underbite providing the relationship of the upper and lower jaw is normal and the canine and premolar teeth on both sides of the mouth are aligned normally. It is faulted however because the teeth are not seated soundly in the mandible. There's insufficient skeletal support underlying the central incisors. Simply put, the central incisors are not well rooted in the jaw bone, therefore more vulnerable to trauma.

Rostral Crossbite

When one or more of the lower incisors are positioned in front of the upper incisors it's referred to as a *Rostral crossbite*. This differs from an underbite because the rostrocaudal relationship of the upper and lower jaw is normal and the canine and premolar teeth on both sides of the mouth are normally aligned in rostral crossbites. Said differently, canine and premolar teeth on both sides of the mouth are normally aligned, but one or more of the lower incisors are positioned in front of the upper incisors when the mouth is closed.

Missing or Extra Teeth

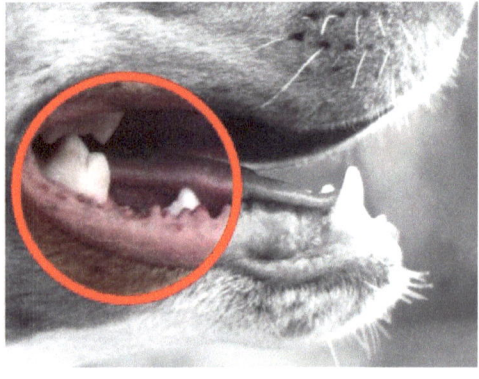

The soundest dentition calls for a full complement of forty-two (42) teeth. Missing premolars are a problem for the most obvious reason: chewing. Extra premolars can be a problem if they cause crowding in the mouth. Extra or supernumerary teeth are genetically linked to missing teeth.

Broken Teeth

Broken teeth or those missing by accident are not penalized because a mechanical injury of this nature cannot be passed on to succeeding generations.

Take Away: Anything other than a normal bite (occlusion/contact between teeth) is detrimental to any breed of dog because it impedes the dog's ability to function without risk of injury.

Dogs with class 2 or class 3 malocclusions, where one jaw is shorter than the other jaw, is most likely due to a genetic trait. Therefore, dogs should not be bred including dogs with an even or level bite.

The Eyes

It is often said that the eyes are the window into the soul. The relationship of the many contributing bones directly influences the shape of the orbit and the eye set, which afford protection to the eye.

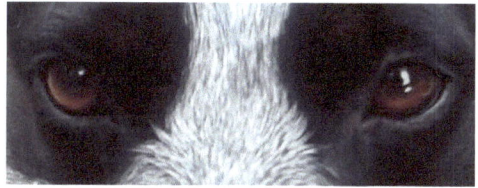

The external shape of the eye is formed by the tissue surrounding the eye rather than the eyeball itself, which is round.

The normal and most practical structure for the eye opening between the eyelids is elongated. Oblique shaped eyelids shield the eyes from dust and wind and other elements because less of the eyeball is exposed.

Due to the lateral placement of their eyes, canines have more peripheral vision than humans or brachycephalic dogs with more frontally positioned eyes. The wider angle allows them to take in a larger overall picture, such as a herding dog looking for sheep in a pasture, a Sighthound scanning the horizon for prey, or a hunting dog looking for birds in the field.

The dog's ability to see close up (binocular overlap) is not as highly developed as is the human eye. That's why it's easier for dogs to catch an object moving sideways than one that is hurled straight at its nose.

Take away: It's natural for dogs to notice fast moving objects in the distance, but not the training treat dropped in the grass under their nose.

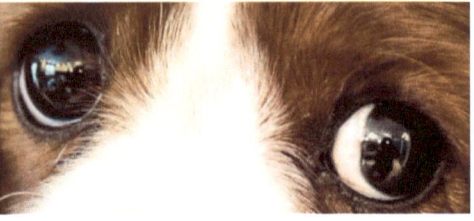

Round, bulging, and sunken small eyes result from an abnormal orbital angle. Due to their shallow orbits, brachycephalic dogs usually have more cornea exposed between the eyelids than dogs with the intermediate mesocephalic and dolichocephalic head varieties. There's a greater chance for serious trauma when the eyes are widely placed with shallow orbits.

The orbitals on brachycephalic heads are positioned more forward than the eyes on intermediate mesocephalic heads that are slightly toward the side.

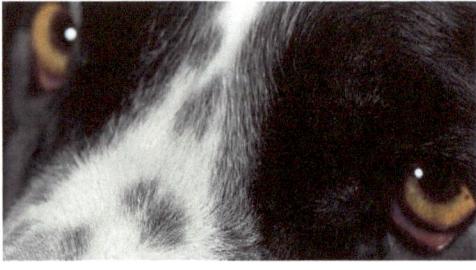

Prominent or visible haws, the third eyelid located in the inside corner of the eye (pictured above), leave the eye vulnerable to injury. A blow to the head can damage the eye, eyelids, muscles or bones surrounding the eyeball.

The Ears

The muscles of the auricle or pinna encompass a dozen separate muscles that control the ear's movement. A dorsal view of the ears with the common muscle of the ear pictured below.

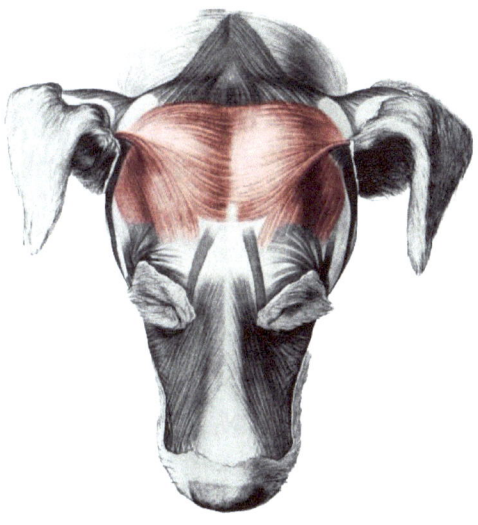

The caudal group rotates the ear laterally and moves the ear opening backwards. The dorsal group elevates the ear and the ventral group lowers the ear, drawing it downward.

The group of muscles at the top of the head toward the dog's nose rotates the ear toward the midline of the head and moves the opening forward (rostral).

When ears are taped or surgically altered to break over, a practice not uncommon in the conformation world, the individual is often unable to lift them for directional movement and properly communicate with people, dogs, or other animals.

Whatever their shape, ears rotate independently to catch and amplify sounds. The ears are also important indicators of emotional responses.

9 Longevity

Belgrave Joe (1868-1888)

The headline read: "**World's Oldest Dog Dies Peacefully at age 30.** Maggie, an Australian Kelpie, lived her days on a dairy farm. And for most of her 30 years of life, she stayed in good health. But she suddenly deteriorated over two days and passed away peacefully in her sleep."

While Maggie might have beat out Bluey by a few months, Bluey, an Australian Cattle dog, was officially the oldest dog of record. He lived for 29 ½ years. His owner bought him as a puppy in 1910 and he grew up to work among sheep and cattle until his passing in 1939.

In 2013, a Beagle-Dachshund-terrier mix named Max, took over the record from Bluey. He was born in 1983 and lived an impressive 29 and 282 days. That's three times the lifespan of the average dog.

The third oldest dog of verifiable record is Butch, a Beagle born in 1975, who lived to the ripe old age of 28 years when he passed in 2003.

Belgrave Joe, a plucky little dog, who lived to 20 years of age weighed 18 pounds and was 16 inches tall. His pedigree was pure hunt terrier, and he is a foundation sire of both Smooth and Wire Fox Terriers.

Breeders can't ignore that genetics play a role in aging and longevity. Dávid Jónás, the author of *A Preliminary Study to Investigate the Genetic Background of Longevity Based on Whole-Genome Sequence Data of Two Methuselah Dogs*, led a team of researchers who sequenced the DNA of two Methuselah, or very old mixed-breed dogs, Kedeves, a 22-year-old female, and Buski, a 27-year-old male, using whole-genome sequencing methods to identify genes that are probably linked to extreme longevity in dogs.

Both dogs lived in rural environments in Hungary and were regularly vaccinated against rabies. Jónás, explained, "Moreover, in dogs, the identification of genes and other genetic loci linked to longevity would enable breeders to select more efficiently for longevity within the breeds."

The Longevity Genes Project, initiated in 1998 at the Albert Einstein College of Medicine by Dr. Nir Barzilai discovered several longevity genes in humans that appear to protect centenarians against major age-related diseases. They found that over 50% of centenarians have some gene in the growth hormone pathways that are affected. They indicated it might be the strongest link to longevity they had seen. It is also highly likely to be inherited from generation to generation.

Growing up with Australian Shepherds, it wasn't unusual to have a healthy and happy 15- or 16-year-old Aussie. Our foundation sire, Hartnagle's Badger, born in 1954, was almost 16 when he went to sleep one sunny afternoon and never woke up. Las Rocosa Christophene and Las Rocosa Sydney were both 16 years of age before they passed. Early on, we always considered longevity one of the main traits for developing our distinct Las Rocosa bloodlines.

Given the definition of extreme longevity; dogs older than 17 years can be considered as dogs of extreme age, much like a human centenarian. A number of our dogs including Las Rocosa Chiquita and Las Rocosa Toms Thunder lived full and healthy lives until they were 18½ years. Gavin Ehringer, the well-known author of the fascinating book, *Leaving the Wild: The Unnatural History of Dogs, Cats, Cows, and Horses,* conveyed, "Tigger, one of my good Las Rocosa Australian Shepherds, lived to be 19½ years. He was put down due to arthritis, or might have made it to 20. He was a blessing to my family." And there are others. Like Las Rocosa Zuni owned by Jane Kerner, a Canadian cattle rancher. She said, "Our little bitch Zuni, a daughter of Champion Las Rocosa Little Wolf, lived to the age of 18. She had a litter at 16 ½. She chewed into the male's kennel from the underside one night when she was determined that we did not know best. She produced twelve puppies who all found good working homes. This was so unexpected, but serendipitous! Anyway, she lived another year thereafter. Zuni was a great dog. She was good natured, an outstanding stockdog and all-around family member!"

There's nothing more heartbreaking as losing that one special dog in your life. Yet, today the average lifespan of companion dogs is only 10 to 13 years. Larger animals tend to live longer than smaller ones, but in dogs, small breeds generally live longer than large breeds because they age more quickly.

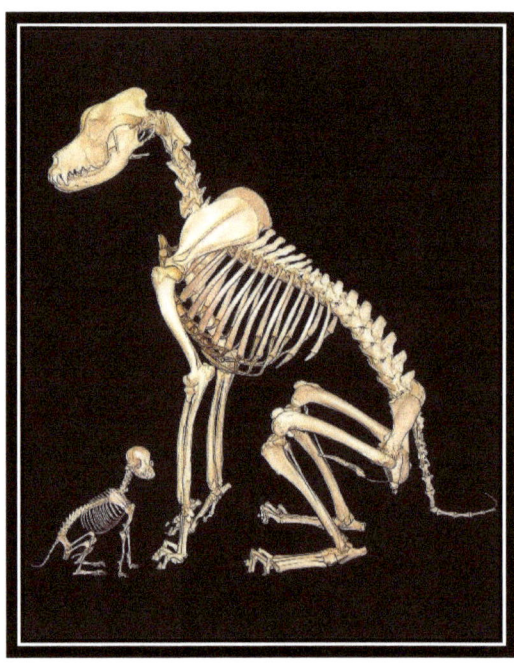

I noticed a trend in Australian Shepherds early on. As individuals from certain bloodlines were being campaigned in the show ring, they were finishing their championships as young, but very mature looking dogs. Interestingly, some of those same dogs were infertile at seven, eight and nine years of age. It was quite surprising.

Our foundation line of Las Rocosa Aussies was and remains slow maturing.

One of the dogs that stood out to me was our Stonehenge Justin Case of Las Rocosa. Justin traced back to original Aussies from which our foundation was built. He was competitive in the show ring, but didn't fill out until he was around seven years of age. Then at age nine, he looked better than ever. The older he got the more handsome he became. On top of that he was sound and in good physical shape throughout his life. He continued to sire puppies and actively work cattle, and did so, until his twilight years.

Health and Hardiness

You can't talk about longevity without discussing a dog's healthspan, which is the length of time a dog enjoys good health. It is important to longevity.

Certain traits, such as long life, fertility and natural whelpers are diminished faster in populations in which natural selection has been relaxed, resulting in a decline in fitness. In other words, less fit individuals are less likely to survive and reproduce than if they are being rigorously tested.

Hardiness is one of the most important traits a lot of the early foundation Australian Shepherds had. They were bred by the yardstick of performance. Most of the early breeders didn't coddle their dogs, so if they weren't healthy— they didn't make it into old age. Or at least they weren't perpetuated. I know it sounds harsh, but it was the reality at that time in history.

Prime Example

When I was a kid my dad gave me a book and a small bronze statue, a replica of the Balto statue in Central Park (top right). It was to honor the Siberian Husky who dependably led a team of sled dogs in the final leg of the 1925 serum run to Nome.

Balto's team faced the worst of the blizzard, which was pounding the region. His team traveled 55 miles almost entirely in the dark and in record sub-zero temperatures. Gunnar Kaasan struggled to keep the sled upright in the blowing snow and 60 to 70 mph wind gusts. Balto never once steered off course.

It wasn't until I was in Alaska, I learned the rest of the story. One that is even more extraordinary. It's about Togo, a Siberian Husky owned by Leonhard Seppala who also bred, raised, and trained Balto. Seppala was known as the "fastest musher in Alaska."

Togo was small for his type, only topping out at about forty-eight pounds with a robust constitution, dense coat of medium length, and strong, sound feet. What Togo lacked in size he made up for in heart. His almond-shaped, tight fitting eyelids gave him excellent protection from the arctic wind and snow. His sire, Suggen, was one of Seppala's great lead dogs. He was a half Siberian husky and half Alaskan Malamute. His dam, Dolly, was a Siberian husky imported to Alaska from Chukchi Inuit stock of Siberia.

Gunnar Kaasen with Balto who faithfully led the team on the final leg of the Great Race of Mercy in 1925.

It was bitterly cold when the deadly diphtheria epidemic swept through the remote town of Nome, Alaska. The nearest supply of diphtheria antitoxin serum was in Anchorage over 1,000 miles away. Delivery by airplane wasn't an option and the remote port into Nome was icebound and unapproachable by steamship. The nearest point the serum could be transported by railway was Nenana. Sled dogs would relay the serum from Nenana and Nome, meeting in the middle at Nulalto. It is a truly remarkable story of courage and fortitude.

Togo in the lead with Leonhard Seppala at the helm.

Seppala was chosen to make the 630-mile round trip from Nome to Nulalto. It was late when he crossed the windswept shorefast ice of Norton Sound, an inlet of the Bering Sea without incident. After crossing, he noticed another dog team. Unbeknownst to Seppala, the epidemic had increased so alarmingly that the officials had decided to speed the serum by adding relays running night and day. He reached the serum after traveling only 170 miles, instead of 315 for which he had originally planned.

When the serum was transferred,

Seppala made the critical decision to go back across Sound with little daylight. He didn't want to have to cross the inlet on the return trip, but the risky shortcut could save a full day of travel and he was in a race for time with the life-saving antidote. The safer alternative would be to follow the land trail all the way around the bay, but it was twice as far. Togo was at loose lead to steer the team around open water. The ice they had crossed the day before had already fragmented and water sprayed up through the cracks. In some places open water was just a few feet away. Togo navigated around the weak spots. Every now and then he put on a burst of speed toward shore. Sometimes blizzard conditions obscured Seppala's ability to see.

The experienced musher was very aware of the dangers. In his writings, he reminisced about an earlier situation on the treacherous sea ice in the windstorm when Seppala heard an ominous crack. He called out to Togo for him to stop, but Togo had felt the ice break and was running at full speed toward the shore. Togo suddenly stopped just short of the shore and reared up in the air to face his team. Seppala was annoyed that his lead dog would act up at such a time, but then he saw the open water about six feet ahead of him. The ice broke. Togo was warning the team. They were stuck on an ice floe that was drifting out to sea. The only thing that Seppala and his dogs could do was wait for the wind to push them back toward land. He bedded the dogs down so they could conserve their energy and hoped the winds would change.

Some hours later, the direction of the wind changed. Togo let out a yip alerting Seppala. The floe drifted toward the sea ice that formed along the coast. In one area, they were only five feet away from the ice, so he decided to attach his towline to Togo throw him to another floe that was jammed against the shoreline. He could only hope that the dog would understand and pull the rest of the team onto land.

When the dog landed, he dug his nails into the sea ice and lunged forward. He was pulling the ice floe, but the towline snapped and fell into the water. Subsequently, when the line snapped, his skill and intelligence went to work. Togo plunged into the frigid water, and seized the line with his jaws, and struggled back out onto the jammed-up floe. Holding the line in his teeth, Togo rolled over the line twice until it was looped around his shoulders, and began to pull. It was his instinct to pull and the floe started to move. Togo continued to pull until it was close enough to the shore for Seppala and his teammates to cross.

The conditions on the return trip were even worse than before. The gale-force winds were deafening. This time the ice held. They made it across. Togo's team, like Balto's team, faced the worst of the blizzard. Seppala found himself in a white-out and limited hours of daylight. Harrowing circumstances made Togo's journey the longest and hardest. He also ran nearly five times as far as any other team. It's also worthy to note the temperature was approximately 30 degrees below zero with wind chill temperatures reaching as low as -85 F.

At times Seppala was unable to see. He trusted Togo's instincts and sense of smell to safely navigate around deadly open stretches of icy water. According to Gay and Laney Salisbury in *The Cruelest Mile*, "He was the best dog [Sepalla] had at navigating shifting fields of ice, and would often run well ahead of the team on a long lead in order to pick out the safest and easiest route across Norton Sound or other parts of the Bering Sea."

But that's only the half of it. That was a noteworthy feat for a dog of any age, but **Togo was 12 years old** when he made the historic dash that frigid January. He led the team over 261 miles of the most perilous part of the serum run, compared to the average of 31 miles each for the other teams. Togo also continued to sire puppies for two more years after that and lived until he was 16 years of age. Seppala said, "I never had a better dog than Togo. His stamina, loyalty, and intelligence could not be improved upon. Togo was the best dog that ever traveled the Alaska trail."

Even though Togo was 12 years of age during the 1925 Serum Run into Nome, he was still fast and strong, a prime example of longevity.

Togo's Sire

Determination is key to developing hardy dogs. In 1914, Seppela entered a race. His team was young and had little experience in difficult conditions. The only veteran was his freight leader, Suggen, a tough dog that was half Siberian and half malamute. The weather was calm and the first forty miles of the race went smoothly.

Then a blizzard kicked up. Seppala was on the summit of Topkok Mountain, and the dogs pushed forward by a strong tailwind, appeared to have lost the trail. Seppala remembered, "By the time we were making it seemed to me that unless I hit the Topkok cabin, we would run a chance of falling over the cliffs which lined the shore." Suddenly, in a lull in the storm, the clouds parted. Seppala saw the cliff was less than 20 feet away. Six hundred feet below that was the Bering Sea. He jumped on the sled brake, but the metal claws only skidded on the hard snow, so he grabbed the steel bar he carried for emergencies.

Salisburys wrote, "He jammed it into a hole in the brake board, then leaned on it with all his weight. The sled came to a stop. The dogs were now facing downward on an icy slope just feet away from the edge of the cliff. The puppies strained to keep from going forward. Still leaning on the bar, Seppala shouted calmly to Suggen over the noise of the wind and ordered him to turn the team around. Suggen growled at the young dogs, but they were reluctant to swing the sled away from the cliff and into the wind."

They said, "Seppala urged the lead dog to force the team around, and Suggen understood the task. He growled again and moved to make the turn. Timidly, then more confidently, the young dogs began to follow, one by one. Suggen leaned into his harnesses, belly close to the ground, as the team clawed its way up the slope." - *The Cruelest Mile*

The dogs had suffered, some had torn pads and broken claws. Others had frostbitten flanks. All were exhausted. Seppala decided he would never again take to the trails when he or his dogs were unfit for the circumstances.

Point of interest: Togo, the Disney movie featured Diesel, a lineal descendant of Togo 14 generations removed who resembled Togo with his agouti coloring.

Side Note: Some of the seemingly unbelievable aspects of the movie are historically accurate, such as when Seppala almost drove the dog team off a cliff. Though the leader of the team in that event was Suggen, Togo's sire.

Longevity in Dogs by Tanya Wheeler

My first Aussie, Las Rocosa Toms Thunder (sired by Las Rocosa Tom Bull Wolf and out of Las Rocosa Riata) lived to be 18 ½ years of age. He was an incredible dog from very old Las Rocosa lines. He was not just an old dog but a dog who reached extraordinary physical agility and physical fitness into his old age, as well.

Las Rocosa Toms Thunder

At 18½ years old, I let him go as a small tumor in his abdomen was growing and I didn't want to see him suffer. I regret I might have let him go sooner. We all know the horrible challenge this type of crisis presents. But until his 18th birthday he was physically capable of walking, trotting, coming up our front steps, which he preferred to the ramp we built almost five years earlier. He never lost his vision and only showed signs of bluing in his eyes in his 18th year. His hearing, however, was a mystery as I felt it was declining at 12 years old, but on times where I would open a tin of dog food, he would appear miraculously before the lid was removed. Selective hearing in dogs is well known but, alas, he did suffer from hearing loss eventually.

As it happened, Tucker was not bred until he was 7 years old. I elected to breed him to a lovely female whose first litter had several of her pups live to ages 15, 16 and 17 years.

There is something to be said, of course, for the longevity of the female, but many of these pups from different dams crossed with Tucker lived with different people, ate different diets, and were exposed to different activities and lifestyles. Yet, they demonstrated the same physical athleticism and longevity they had seemingly inherited.

Longevity is also likely linked to structural integrity. Although much has changed in the almost 30 years since Tucker was born in 1993, cancer seems to be the predominantly common killer of dogs today. While many of Tucker's descendants have shown the propensity for longevity, there have been a couple with cancer, which, incidentally, were from the same household. Fortunately, they survived and went on to live to 15 and 16 years old. Many others have lived longer without health concerns throughout their entire lives.

So, what is the importance of longevity? Whether it is a genetic predisposition, quality of life, diet, fitness level, or mental stimulation—quality of life in so many areas—it would be hard to isolate. It does beg the question: How does this play a role in preserving dogs who demonstrate longevity?

If we can breed dogs to not only live longer, but live longer as physically healthy, active old dogs, why would we not consider this an important selection criterion for breeding?

Alternatively, some will argue that longevity has more to do with diet, exercise, and lifestyle. I would agree this plays a critical role. At the same time, studies have proven that DNA can be altered by the environment. Research in humans has shown a likely genetic link to longevity, with the risk of acquiring age-related disease being postponed. If dogs possess this similar genetic link for longevity, then it's definitely something we should select for along with a lower incidence of age-related disease that might occur earlier in lives of breeding dogs. How do we select for this when the average breeding age for dogs is probably between three and six years old? This is too early to assess longevity in the individual. However, a long look at not only the parents but the siblings longevity can offer some clues.

While no dog lives forever, there are some who manage to live very healthy lives—longer than others who will exhibit age-related disease prematurely. Genetic health screening today is helpful in determining some heritable traits we know can bring on early diseases. However, it doesn't explain everything that can go wrong. For example, epilepsy, immune mediated disease, and cancer are some of the least understood diseases that result in early health issues. We do understand there may be a genetic or inherited component to epilepsy and even some cancers that are more common in dogs, but we do not yet have enough knowledge to help us carefully select against these horrible fates.

Longevity, which is likely inherited to some degree, is still a positive criterion that you might want to select for in breeding better dogs. While longevity in itself may not be a criterion that can be identified with a gene or genetic combination mutation, it has the property of providing a longer, healthier life than those individuals who do not possess this trait. So making a statement that you want to breed this dog now before she's too old because her dad only lived to 10 years old—might not be the best criteria. And, yes, I did hear that once.

> With longevity, you have an animal who, for whatever reason, has outlived other animals, and may possibly have the genetic propensity to be more resistant to disease, or whose genetic makeup is more stable and less likely to be susceptible to mutation. Therefore, if you have a dog who is still active and healthy at 10, 12, or 15 years old, something is at work that allows the individual to thrive.

We all wish our dogs would live longer. The only time I heard a reasonable argument against longevity is when working dogs became deaf and less useful on a working livestock operation, and the rancher argued reasonably that all the physical athleticism in the world doesn't help if they are stone deaf. I guess there is some merit in that, but most working dogs that make it to the hearing loss age—10 or 12 years or older—should not need much direction to execute their job!

Longevity, I believe, will continue to be included in the vast criteria I value when breeding my dogs so that others may experience the job of a very old, very happy dog.

Thoughts from Michael J. Ryan

Over nearly fifty years of friendship, Jeanne Joy Hartnagle-Taylor and I have engaged in endless hours of discussion in reference to the structure of dogs. Usually, this was specifically in reference to Australian Shepherds, but inevitably branched out into many other breeds. With our shared background in livestock and horses, we also incorporated elements of those species. Some of these discussions were in person, in private, in public, on the telephone, and often with the participation, or contributions from endless others in the dog and animal world. We challenged traditional thinking, incorporated traditional thinking, and over time began to recognize and trust our own observations and views. These were not simply opinions garnered through a participation in some competitive aspect of the dog world, but were the result of endless study and real-world experience. Jeanne's father Ernest Hartnagle was often part of our discussions and was known to make the statement, "Don't tell me, show me." *Canine Form Follows Function* is very much in keeping with that guidance.

Relating Form to Function: It is easy to lay claim to specific beliefs in the world of dogdom. A common comment would go something like this, "I like a smooth extended trot that could go all day." But wait, can a smooth extended trot really go all day? If that were the case, why don't the wild canids that really do go all day not have that long sweeping side gait? Is nature deceiving us? More angulation requires more muscle. More muscle lends itself to greater fatigue. In my real herding dogs, fatigue is a critical issue. Herding breed dogs with excessive mass are not suited to the task for which they were originally intended. Real herding dogs are not primarily trial dogs that only have to hold up for a fist full of minutes during competition, or breed ring dogs that trot around a ring. For real herding dogs, excessive mass is a genuine concern.

The Blueprint: An overview of the "architecture" or structure of the dog is essential to the understanding of a given individual, family, breed, or grouping of dogs, and where their shared traits will find strength, weakness, and suitability to purpose. A nice illustration of this suitability to purpose is the locking mechanism in a horse's stifle (knee) that allows the horse to sleep standing up. Then, how this corresponds to structures further down the leg is a strong illustration of how different parts influence one another. The dog's ability to dig in with its feet is a more subtle example, but also shows how given dogs may be better suited to specific tasks because of something so specific as the shape of their feet.

Dog Architecture: Undoubtedly, discussing the "Blueprint" of specific breeds invokes the most potential controversy. However, when this discussion is applied to the actual canines that are employing their structure successfully, the evidence speaks for itself. This discussion is not a battle between "show" dogs and "working" dogs. It is a discussion of what works best for the intended purpose of the respective breeds. Both Jeanne Joy and I have competed in the breed ring (show ring), on the trial field, and in the trial arena. It is all a lot of fun for the people who choose these sports. What is discussed here is how to view the correctness of dogs for their intended purposes, and how to interpret those standards that attempt to describe breeds as they become more standardized. The extended trot of the German Shepherd Dog is not correct for the Australian Shepherd. While they are both herding dogs, the kind of herding that they do is not the same. The GSD is a trotting breed while the Australian Shepherd is a sprinting breed. With that in mind, reflect back to the earlier discussion of the racing Greyhound versus the show Greyhound. Different functions favor different forms.

I can also share that as both Jeanne Joy and I have watched the Australian Shepherd evolve, we have seen Australian Shepherds with both a sprinting structure and the corresponding shorter side gait at the trot. We have also seen Australian Shepherds with a trotting structure, or longer side gait at the trot. Often dogs with the longer side gait will run with a rocking horse like motion. When dogs with a shorter side gait break into a full sprint, it is usually a smoother transition. Many herding dog enthusiasts have found the "rocking horse" sprint to be unsettling to the stock. This is particularly true with sheep that live on the range or in large fields where they are not worked by a wide variety of dogs. Coyotes, wolves, cape hunting dogs, and other wild canids that actually hunt for survival do not exhibit the "rocking horse" sprint. They are generally shorter gaited with a smooth transition to the sprint. The unsettling gait would not serve their purpose. The herding breeds that have a more similar structure tend to be less unsettling to the stock. This has been my own experience and the experience and observation of many herding dog professionals. Having gained this understanding myself, I have to agree with Jeanne Joy's discussion in, "The Blueprint."

Neck Topline and the Body: So many discussions of the dog's neck, topline, and body seem to fall in the category of what is aesthetically pleasing, when in fact these are critical structures that influence the dog's ability to perform a given task. Observing that a dog may appear to be "short necked" may tell us more about the structural attachments and angulation of the forequarters than it does about the length of the dog's neck. It is helpful that Jeanne Joy addresses those aspects. In the breed ring dogs are often on a tight leash where they are strung up to have a regal appearance. Judging the Australian Shepherd breed, I have often asked dogs to be gaited on a loose leash. For real working Australian Shepherds, Kelpies, Border Collies, and others, the dog's most efficient gait is with the head lowered. This allows the dog to work over its center of gravity more effectively and accommodate changes in what the job requires relevant to the stock or to the terrain. Neither of these factors are typically considerations in the breed ring.

Anecdotally, I am reminded of a visit from a good friend. She had come a long way from out of state and was generously taking pictures of my Australian Shepherds and Border Collies working sheep. She was taking pictures of an Aussie female and told me that she was about to ask me what the hump was in my dog's back when she remembered what I had said about dogs dropping their heads in working situations. The hump was the dog's shoulders. This particular Aussie would not only drop her head to be level with her back while working, but would also frequently drop her head below the level of her shoulders. This made the shoulders look like a hump. There was nothing abnormal about this dog's structure, as a matter of fact, she was quite correct. She was simply using her head and neck effectively as part of her balance and movement. The dog scaling the embankment is using its head and neck in a similar manner.

In discussions about a dog's croup, some would conclude that this is a matter of breed preference or personal taste. That couldn't be further from the truth. The muscular and skeletal structures of the croup are critical elements of a dog's effective movement. Jeanne illustrates that these structural elements contribute to power and the thrust of movement in the sprinting dog. The angle of the croup and its muscling are also important to sudden changes of direction allowing a dog to pull up under itself and pivot. A flatter croup does not make the same accommodation.

The Forequarters: Understanding the forequarters of a dog is so much more than can be contained in a few paragraphs. There are a few points that stand out strongly to me. First of all, referring to a certain type of foot as a, "modified hare-foot," is sure to draw attention. For many the use of the term, "hare-foot," implies that the foot is faulty. This is not the case in reference to the way that the term is used in this discussion. A hare-foot is simply an elongated foot where the two center toes are longer than the outside toes. It is essentially the opposite of a cat-foot that is round and compact with shorter toes. Therefore, the modified hare-foot describes a paw that is neither of these extremes.

A pet peeve of my own is brought up in this section of the book. Feet in dogs are very important. It has been my experience to be questioned about my placement of dogs in some very prestigious judging assignments. Ringside experts have questioned the low placing of dogs with beautiful side gaits, exquisite heads, and so forth. They have even asked me if there was something wrong with the dog's dentition. If they have any regard for my opinion at all, they are certain that it is something that cannot be seen from ring side. Very often it is bad feet.

The best show participants are wise to do an impeccable job of grooming a dog's paws. And on the other hand, wise judges will be careful to look past the grooming. Anyone who has depended on dogs in a hard-working capacity will sooner or later learn the importance of a well-structured foot. "No foot, no dog" is not just a catchy phrase. It is real life. Weak pads that slip and bleed render a herding, hunting, or sledding dog almost useless. Splayed feet that are constantly injured and ripping the webbing between the toes are a sad state of affairs. The foot that has poorly arched toes is always injured. If you really need a dog, weak and faulty feet can be an unfortunate let down.

An accomplished dog woman that I know is one of the people who questioned my placement in a breed class. As I respect this woman, we engaged in a lengthy discussion of dog conformation. My background in livestock and horses causes me to interpret the dog's breed standard from the perspective of the original intended purpose of the breed. Horses, cattle, pigs, goats, and sheep all have to have good feet. Everything falls apart if they have bad feet. It became apparent that this woman was able to follow my judging very closely for the most part and understood my placements. However, there were a few times when she really couldn't follow why I had placed a given dog so low in the class. After our lengthy discourse, it became clear that those dogs had bad feet. The next time that she watched me judge, our placements were even closer. This woman has used dogs in many fields of competition and in many capacities. She knows the importance of good feet.

In herding dog competitions, I have known many dogs to have injured feet take them out of competition. It is interesting to note that often it is the same dog or family of dogs that are getting injured and withdrawn from competition. Sometimes an injury is just an injury. In other cases, it is the result of poorly conformed feet. While it is common for people in the show ring to take elements of conformation to an extreme, it is also common for people in performance areas, such as herding, to almost dismiss the importance of conformation. For the well-being of the dogs, conformation does matter. Feet are probably one of the most important aspects of dog conformation in the discussion of *Canine Form Follows Function*.

It is possible that I have said more about the canine foot that is proportionate to Jeanne's section on the forequarters. Obviously, the rear quarters also have feet! It is just that feet are so often overlooked, so very critical to a real using dog, and so very illustrative of the purpose of this book.

In other aspects of the forequarters I appreciate how Jeanne Joy has connected each of the anatomical parts of the dog to its intended purpose. This guides the reader into understanding what is actually important to the well-being of the dog as opposed to the aesthetic leanings of people's preferences.

There are people in the wide world of dogdom who will single out a given element of dog structure and elevate that feature above all others, or above the dog's structure in its entirety. This is faulty thinking. A single feature can be completely disabling. One should never lose track of the whole in favor of a single part. Jeanne Joy demonstrates that faulty reasoning in her discussion of the forty-five degree layback of shoulder in the Australian Shepherd. At one point in time this was the most important point of structure discussed by breeders and those who competed in the breed. People believed that specific shoulder angulation was critical in the breed ring and in herding performance and competition. That thinking is largely disproven now, but the influence of that discussion lives on in the breed.

With all of this said about the forequarters, it seems that a single feature can be disabling, but one should never lose track of the whole. Everything in dog structure is connected to everything. The overall assembly of the forequarters is important in both its specificity and in its entirety.

The Hindquarters: Again, it is apparent in the discussion of the hindquarters that all of the parts of a dog's anatomy are inextricably linked. Changes in one area will influence and change other areas. If we indulge in faulty thinking and apply it to our breeding practices or in the way that we employ dogs, that faulty thinking will impact the very dogs that we hold in such high regard.

It is of particular interest that whether it be dogs or horses, nature works to maintain balance in relationship to the parts of the dog. Perhaps we would be wisest to hear this message. Balance between the respective parts of dog anatomy is paramount. More simply put, balance supersedes exaggerations. It is not my intent to belittle or berate any specific breeds of dogs, but any knowledgeable dog person can cite breeds that have chosen to exaggerate various features to the detriment of the very breed that they love.

When Jeanne Joy addresses these elements in the hindquarters of the dog, we can better understand where something goes wrong. Cow hocks have been tolerated in specific breeds of horses and dogs. While the total picture is still more important than a single feature, I would not excuse cow hocks out of hand. It is a feature that must be factored into one's use of the dog and into one's breeding practices. It is an excellent example of what this author is telling us.

I would be remiss if I did not make an additional comment about the rear feet of the dog. The illustration of poorly developed plantar pads and loose ligaments that Jeanne Joy offers on page 79 is a shining example of what should not be tolerated. This is detrimental to the real-life performance of herding, hunting, and draft dogs. Too many dogs in the breed ring and on the performance field exhibit this fault and too many competitors and breed ring judges are oblivious to it. Repeatedly, I have seen dogs with this type of rear feet slip their pads and rip the webbing between their toes. Of course, many dogs will never be asked to perform in their originally intended roles and the problem will never come to be recognized. It is still important. Also, as we remember how nature works to maintain balance in the total makeup of the dog, it is likely that the front feet of the dog will also be compromised. One would be well advised to take this into consideration if a dog is going to be asked to perform any rigorous task. With respect to people who show their dogs, most of them would not want to promote a feature that could be detrimental to their dogs either. Breed ring judges should simply know better than to promote such weakness, but that is an editorial comment that runs astray of what I was asked to contribute to this text.

The overarching outlook represented in this portion of the book discusses many known structural elements. Ms. Hartnagle-Taylor has made a strong effort to link structure to performance. My previous paragraphs try to bring to the forefront some of the kinds of thinking that should happen as we attempt to apply this knowledge.

The Gait: "As a dog moves, so is it built." I don't know who the famous person is that originally said this or who may have adapted it from somewhere else and applied it to the dog, but I do believe that there is a strong element of truth in this expression. Jeanne and I have discussed the gait of herding dogs for as long as we have known one another. When we were younger, we were more inclined to accept popular thinking, but with greater knowledge one is inclined to challenge what comes to be popular thinking. This is especially true because we both found ourselves in the presence of real working dogs. The structure of these real working dogs was typically not consistent with commonly held beliefs.

There are very strong tendencies within the breeds that evolved for real herding. If the task was similar, the structure of the dogs that were successfully performing that task tended to be similar. One of the best examples would be the proportion and structure of Australian Kelpies, hill Border Collies, and range working Australian Shepherds. None of these dogs are inclined to have the extreme angulation. All of them are expected to perform in rugged and varied terrain and with difficult livestock. Initially, none were selectively bred for a specific look, but for a specific task. That task dictated the structure that would be successful.

Examining those elements of structure warranted further study. The author and I both pursued a deeper understanding. In this book Jeanne has carefully considered the elements of anatomy and motion. As she compiled that information, it became my mantra to look at the wild canids that effectively preyed on the same species that our herding dogs worked. Clearly, there are strong parallels between the real herding dogs and their wild cousins, the coyotes and wolves.

Instead of accepting popular beliefs that appeal to competition in the show ring, we may do well to consider the standard of perfection that has been established in nature. An efficient and effective gait may be more consistent with the wild cousins of the dog.

The Head: The head of each breed is so distinctive. Some of the slight variances that become extremely important to some breeders and breeds are probably not nearly as critical to the well-being of the dogs themselves. The discussion that I enjoy most in this section of Jeanne Joy's book is the distinction between the three head types. It is my personal belief that the intermediate type is best suited to the kind of herding dogs that I work with. I see specific drawbacks to shorter and blunter heads and do not believe that they are well adapted to the work that I expect to get from my dogs. Specifically, I would guard against features that allow injuries to the eyes, such as bulging eyes and loose haws. The longer and narrower heads may not have so much susceptibility to injury in the same way as the shorter heads, but I wonder if the slighter bone and muscling in those longer heads would not be more exposed to impact injuries such as hooves and horns.

Jeanne's more thorough going discussion of the dog's dentition is valuable. Most discussions that I have heard in the dog world center on the issue of undershot and overshot bites and counting teeth. Both of these are genuine concerns for dogs, but there is significantly more to a dog's dentition. The wry bite and each of the other variances that are brought forward, play into the well-being of canine dentition.

As in all other aspects of a successfully functioning dog, we must remember to keep everything in perspective. Simply finding faults in dogs is not the answer. Sometimes it is more important to view canine structure in its entirety and focus on individual faults only insofar as they impact the dog's intended function. A single fault can sometimes truly be disabling, but that is usually not the case.

This book emphasizes that we need to be knowledgeable of canine form and function. We also need to understand the intended function of the dog as thoroughly as possible. It should not be the case that the dogs truly performing the breed's intended purpose are seen as lesser individuals. They should be the population that offers us a perspective through which to view the breed. In our selection of dogs for human's purposes I think that we need to also look at the wild canines and the selections that nature has made. Jeanne Joy Hartnagle-Taylor has put together a very nice connection between form and function. She has made a great case for balance in canine form. With that in mind I would like to conclude with a loose interpretation of a quote from Aristotle, "Perfection is not found in the extremes, but in the balance of things." ~ Michael J. Ryan

International ASCA Senior, Breeder Judge, Lifelong stockman from a long line of stockmen; A successful trial competitor in ASCA and USBCHA; a former AHBA Judge and AKC competitor, but most importantly, a man who has used herding dogs in a wide range of livestock settings.

Insight from Carol Ann Hartnagle

In her latest work, Jeanne Joy Hartnagle-Taylor presents updated and easy-to-understand information for evaluating the conformation of the performance dog – *to enhance or enable top functionality*. Amateur and professional dog trainers, breeders, and judges will all benefit from her insights based on recognizing correct structure for purpose.

In athletics as in architecture, form follows function. Nowhere is that truth more important than in the real world of canine performance and canine performance sports. The better a dog's conformation…how the animal measures up to, or "conforms," to the original and functional standards of its breed or type…the better it will be able to perform its **intended** function.

Using manifold photographs and drawings, this masterful work will show you how to develop the "eye" that any dog owner needs to assess canine conformation and anatomy. Its comprehensive text focuses on ideal and abnormal conformation features; balance and symmetry; the relationship between conformation faults and athletic ability as well as anatomical elements, structural flaws and the relationship between structure and function.

The way a dog is physically built, his conformation, tells a lot about the original function, sport, or discipline for which he is best suited. With a well-trained eye, you can see his strengths and his weaknesses, and therefore determine how you train him, on which areas to focus, the techniques best chosen to improve his skills, and methods that should be used (or avoided) to maintain your dog's health and soundness.

Having seen first-hand performance dogs in all manners of sport and real-world tasks, I continue to be in awe of the physical demands we place on our canine companions. Tasked even harder are those structures not configured for those challenges. Many of the dogs do not lack instinct, talent or desire. However, they often lack the proper structure to do certain tasks efficiently. For example, I've seen a number of herding dogs in competition unable to run fast enough to the head of a group of livestock to stop the flow of motion or turn in time to maneuver a gate or chute efficiently. These dogs wear down (muscle fatigue) and experience irregular bone wear and cartilage tears. Not surprisingly, we see the most capable dogs for a sport – properly trained, in proper condition <u>and</u> correctly conformed for that task - are those who excel.

In sport or in real working environments, it is true as the athletic demands of the owner increase, there is a proportional increase in the physical demands placed upon the dog's body. These increased demands placed upon the dog introduce a higher risk of injury. It is in this vein to approach the content and consider when selecting dogs for their utility, first remember its intended function. ~ Carol Ann Hartnagle

A multi-disciplined AKC and ASCA judge; international breed mentor; co-author of *The Total Australian Shepherd; The Miniature American Shepherd Judging Analysis*; owner/breeder and handler of the world class Hall of Fame Kennel, Hartnagle's Las Rocosa Aussies established in 1955.

 # Illustrations

 # About the Author

Images provided by The National Academy of Sciences, Veterinary Dental College, Gary Anderson Photography, Hartnagle Family Archive, Sue Bishop, Richard Bruner, Jennifer Cannon, Terri Carver, Beth Crandall, Bruce Dale, Kay Delk-Keziah, Herrmann Dittrich, Marianne Dwight, Louis Agassiz Fuertes, Maj. J. C. Gotwals (Sigrid Seppala Hanks Collection), Benjamin Waterhouse Hawkins, Jim Hartnagle, Michaela Hejlová, Ashlyn Hunt, Tosha Hunt/Aston Creek Photography, Percy T. Jones, Silja Jonsson, George Goodwin Kilburne, Kati Kuuttila, Paul Libby, Tracy Libby, Anne Martin, Terry Martin, Edwin Megargee, Edward Hebert Miner, Heidi Mobley, Edmund Osthaus, Lynne Ouchida, JP Norris, Lynda Oleksuk, Rich Ruddish, Linda Shaw, Joe Sheeron, Mekenna Smith, Katy Lynn Taylor, Veronika Tvrdá, Daniela Van der Lichte, Dorien Vogelaar, Robert F. Way, VMD, MS, Walter A. Weber, Tanya Wheeler, Faye Unrau, inspiration from Monika Zagrobelna, Zing Pix (Jeff Jaquish).

Jeanne Joy Hartnagle-Taylor comes from a lifetime association with working stockdogs in demanding situations on ranches in the real world. She is an ASCA Senior Breeder Conformation Judge, Stockdog and Herding Trial Judge, and breeding authority. In partnership with her family, they developed a distinct bloodline of Australian Shepherds that are recognized around the world under the name, Hartnagle's Las Rocosa Aussies. They earned the distinction of becoming ASCA's number one Hall of Fame Kennel, Hall of Fame Excellent Kennel and ASCA's Stockdog Kennel of Excellence. They are sound, healthy dogs proven by the yardstick of performance in the real world.

If you like **Canine Form Follows Function: Separating Fact From Fiction** you are sure to like: The Australian Shepherd Judging Compendium.

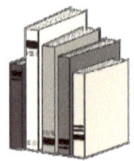

Other books by the author:

All About Aussies: The Australian Shepherd from A to Z

All About Aussies: The Complete Handbook on Australian Shepherds

Greasepaint Matadors: The Unsung Heroes of Rodeo

Have You Ever Wondered? The Difference Between…

The Australian Shepherd Judging Compendium

The Miniature American Shepherd Judging Analysis

Stockdog Savvy

Stockdog Savvy ASCA Title Tracker

Stockdog Savvy AKC Title Tracker

Stockdog Savvy AHBA Title Tracker

Stockdog Savvy CKC Title Tracker

Stockdog Savvy Multi-Venue Title Tracker

Stockdog Savvy Training Journal

The Stockdog Savvy Training Journal

The Stockdog Savvy Workbook

Stockdog Training Journal

The Australian Shepherd

Judging Compendium

by Jeanne Joy Hartnagle-Taylor

If we stop looking at the Australian Shepherd through the lens of its original purpose as a working stockdog, we will have created (in time) a distinctly different breed.

"The text is easy to read and carefully written with a good analysis of unique traits that are described in the breed standard. The illustrations of each trait give the reader good insight into why the breed standard requires certain body proportions and what is considered correct breed type, movement and character. I would recommend this judging compendium to anyone who is seriously interested in a better understanding of the Australian Shepherd breed."

~ Dr. Carmen L. Battaglia

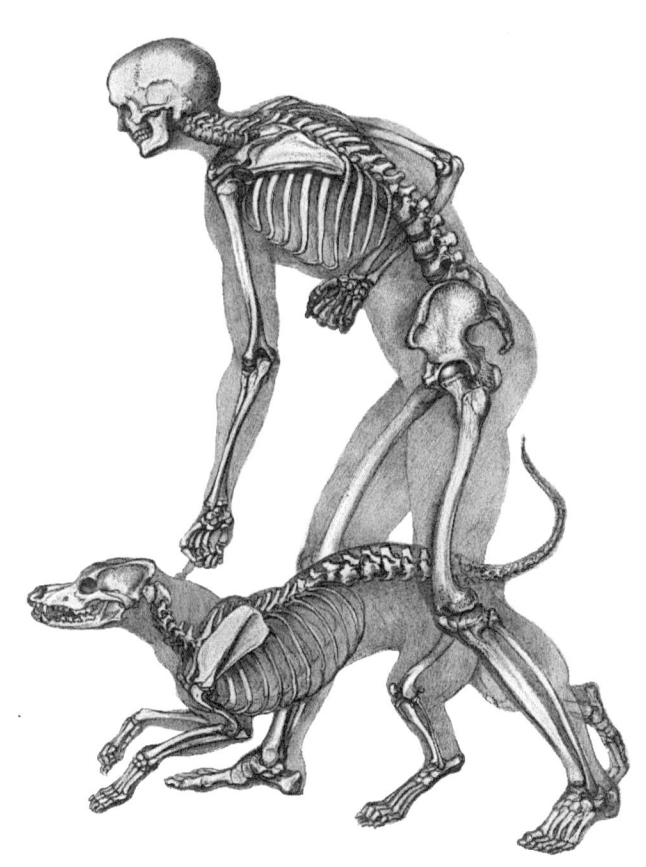

www.ingramcontent.com/pod-product-compliance
Lightning Source LLC
Chambersburg PA
CBHW041553220426
43666CB00003B/53